Paul de Man is to many a driving force behind the critical movement of deconstruction. To others, he is a scandalous figure, due to the posthumous exposure of his involvement with the collaborationist press in Second World War Belgium. Whatever the 'truth' about de Man, his work is essential reading. This guide offers a way in to the full range of his work, from the critical essays to the wartime journalism.

Martin McQuillan explores and contextualises such crucial ideas as:

- literary language and critical misreading
- deconstruction and the impossible
- autobiography and disfiguration
- aesthetic ideology

For those seeking a wide-ranging, non-partisan introduction to Paul de Man, this is the book to choose.

**Martin McQuillan** is a Lecturer in Cultural Theory and Analysis at the University of Leeds. He is the editor of Routledge's *Narrative Reader* and co-author of *Deconstructing Disney*.

# ROUTLEDGE CRITICAL THINKERS
*essential guides for literary studies*

Series Editor: Robert Eaglestone, Royal Holloway, University of London

*Routledge Critical Thinkers* is a series of accessible introductions to key figures in contemporary critical thought.

With a unique focus on historical and intellectual contexts, each volume examines a key theorist's:

- significance
- motivation
- key ideas and their sources
- impact on other thinkers

Concluding with extensively annotated guides to further reading, *Routledge Critical Thinkers* are the literature student's passport to today's most exciting critical thought.

Already available:
*Fredric Jameson* by Adam Roberts
*Jean Baudrillard* by Richard J. Lane
*Paul de Man* by Martin McQuillan
*Sigmund Freud* by Pamela Thurschwell
*Edward Said* by Bill Ashcroft and Pal Ahluwalia
*Maurice Blanchot* by Ullrich Haase and William Large

Forthcoming:
*Judith Butler*
*Frantz Fanon*

For further details on this series, see www.literature.routledge.com/rct

# PAUL DE MAN

*Martin McQuillan*

London and New York

First published 2001
by Routledge
11 New Fetter Lane, London EC4P 4EE

Simultaneously published in the USA and Canada
by Routledge
29 West 35th Street, New York, NY 10001

*Routledge is an imprint of the Taylor & Francis Group*

Typeset in Perpetua by Taylor & Francis Books Ltd
Printed and bound in Great Britain by Clays Ltd, St Ives plc

*British Library Cataloguing in Publication Data*
A catalogue record for this book is available from the British Library

*Library of Congress Cataloging in Publication Data*
McQuillan, Martin.
  Paul de Man / Martin McQuillan
  p. cm. – (Routledge critical thinkers)
  Includes bibliographical references and index.
  1. De Man, Paul–Contributions in criticism. 2. Deconstruction. I. Title. II. Series.
PN75.D45 M45 2001
801'.95'092–dc21                                                        00-062795

ISBN 0–415–21512–9 (hbk)
ISBN 0–415–21513–7 (pbk)

# CONTENTS

# SERIES EDITOR'S PREFACE

The books in this series offer introductions to major critical thinkers who have influenced literary studies and the humanities. The *Routledge Critical Thinkers* series provides the books you can turn to first when a new name or concept appears in your studies.

Each book will equip you to approach a key thinker's original texts by explaining her or his key ideas, putting them into context and, perhaps most importantly, showing you why this thinker is considered to be significant. The emphasis is on concise, clearly written guides which do not presuppose a specialist knowledge. Although the focus is on particular figures, the series stresses that no critical thinker ever existed in a vacuum but, instead, emerged from a broader intellectual, cultural and social history. Finally, these books will act as a bridge between you and the thinker's original texts: not replacing them but rather complementing what she or he wrote.

These books are necessary for a number of reasons. In his 1997 autobiography, *Not Entitled*, the literary critic Frank Kermode wrote of a time in the 1960s:

On beautiful summer lawns, young people lay together all night, recovering from their daytime exertions and listening to a troupe of Balinese musicians. Under their blankets or their sleeping bags, they would chat drowsily about the gurus of the time. ... What they repeated was largely hearsay; hence my lunchtime suggestion, quite impromptu, for a series of short, very cheap books offering authoritative but intelligible introductions to such figures.

There is still a need for 'authoritative and intelligible introductions'. But this series reflects a different world from the 1960s. New thinkers have emerged and the reputations of others have risen and fallen, as new research has developed. New methodologies and challenging ideas have spread through the arts and humanities. The study of literature is no longer – if it ever was – simply the study and evaluation of poems, novels and plays. It is also the study of the ideas, issues, and difficulties which arise in any literary text and in its interpretation. Other arts and humanities subjects have changed in analogous ways.

With these changes, new problems have emerged. The ideas and issues behind these radical changes in the humanities are often presented without reference to wider contexts or as theories which you can simply 'add on' to the texts you read. Certainly, there's nothing wrong with picking out selected ideas or using what comes to hand – indeed, some thinkers have argued that this is, in fact, all we can do. However, it is sometimes forgotten that each new idea comes from the pattern and development of somebody's thought and it is important to study the range and context of their ideas. Against theories 'floating in space', the *Routledge Critical Thinkers* series places key thinkers and their ideas firmly back in their contexts.

More than this, these books reflect the need to go back to the thinker's own texts and ideas. Every interpretation of an idea, even the most seemingly innocent one, offers its own 'spin', implicitly or explicitly. To read only books on a thinker, rather than texts by that thinker, is to deny yourself a chance of making up your own mind. Sometimes what makes a significant figure's work hard to approach is not so much its style or content as the feeling of not knowing where to start. The purpose of these books is to give you a 'way in' by offering an accessible overview of a these thinkers' ideas and works and by guiding your further reading, starting with each thinker's own texts. To use a metaphor from the philosopher Ludwig Wittgenstein (1889–1951), these books are ladders, to be thrown away after you have climbed to the next level. Not only, then, do they equip you to approach new ideas, but also they empower you, by leading you back to a theorist's own texts and encouraging you to develop your own informed opinions.

Finally, these books are necessary because, just as intellectual needs have changed, the education systems around the world – the contexts in which introductory books are usually read – have changed radically, too. What was suitable for the minority higher education system of the 1960s is not suitable for the larger, wider, more diverse, high technology education systems of the 21st century. These changes call not just for new, up-to-date, introductions but new methods of presentation. The presentational aspects of *Routledge Critical Thinkers* have been developed with today's students in mind.

Each book in the series has a similar structure. They begin with a section offering an overview of the life and ideas of each thinker and explain why she or he is important. The central section of each book discusses the thinker's key ideas, their context, evolution and reception. Each book concludes with a survey of the thinker's impact, outlining how their ideas have been taken up and developed by others. In addition, there is a detailed final section suggesting and describing books for further reading. This is not a 'tacked-on' section but an integral part of each volume. In the first part of this section you will find brief descriptions of the thinker's key works: following this, information on the most useful critical works and, in some cases, on relevant websites. This section will guide you in your reading, enabling you to follow your interests and develop your own projects. Throughout each book, references are given in what is known as the Harvard system (the author and the date of works cited are given in the text and you can look up the full details in the bibliography at the back). This offers a lot of information in very little space. The books also explain technical terms and use boxes to describe events or ideas in more detail, away from the main emphasis of the discussion. Boxes are also used at times to highlight definitions of terms frequently used or coined by a thinker. In this way, the boxes serve as a kind of glossary, easily identified when flicking through the book.

The thinkers in the series are 'critical' for three reasons. First, they are examined in the light of subjects which involve criticism: principally literary studies or English and cultural studies, but also other disciplines which rely on the criticism of books, ideas, theories and unquestioned assumptions. Second, they are critical because studying their work will provide you with a 'tool kit' for your own informed critical reading and thought, which will make you critical. Third, these thinkers are critical because they are crucially important: they deal with ideas and questions which can overturn conventional understandings of the world, of texts, of everything we take for granted, leaving us with a deeper understanding of what we already knew and with new ideas.

No introduction can tell you everything. However, by offering a way into critical thinking, this series hopes to begin to engage you in an activity which is productive, constructive and potentially life-changing.

# ACKNOWLEDGEMENTS

Rousseau writes in the 'Essay on the Origin of Language', 'in order not to find me in contradiction with myself, I should be allowed enough time to explain myself'. An introduction, of this sort, to the complexity of de Man is by definition a contradiction. One day I hope to leave my students a fuller explanation. I would like to thank all those who discussed aspects of this book with me, including: Eleanor Byrne, Peter Buse, Nuria Triana-Toribio, Stephan Herbrechter, Phil Rothsfield, Roland Munro, Laurent Milesi, Peggy Kamuf, and Julian Wolfreys. I would especially like to thank Liz Brown for her patience and editorial skills and Robert Eaglestone who taught me that most things which are impossible were invented in the eighteenth century. This book is dedicated to Professor Shaun Richards and the Literature Field at Staffordshire University, 1997–2000, in gratitude for their friendship, intellectual and social.

# ABBREVIATIONS

Throughout this book, references to the following texts by Paul de Man are abbreviated as follows:

AI     *Aesthetic Ideology*, ed. Andrzej Warminski, (Minneapolis: University of Minnesota Press, 1996).

AR    *Allegories of Reading: Figural Language in Rousseau, Nietzsche, Rilke, and Proust* (New Haven and London: Yale University Press, 1979).

BI     *Blindness and Insight: Essays in the Rhetoric of Contemporary Criticism*, 2nd edition (Minneapolis: University of Minnesota Press, 1983).

RR    *The Rhetoric of Romanticism* (New York: Columbia University Press, 1984).

RT    *The Resistance to Theory* (Minneapolis: University of Minnesota Press, 1986).

For all other references the Harvard System is used; full bibliographical details may be found in the Works Cited section of this book.

# WHY DE MAN?

Paul de Man died of cancer in 1983 at the relatively early age of sixty-four. Towards the end of those sixty-four years he had begun to emerge as a literary critic and philosophical thinker of international standing. At his memorial service the French philosopher Jacques Derrida described his friend's achievement as a transformation of 'the field of literary theory, revitalising all the channels that irrigate it both inside and outside the university, in the United States and Europe' (Derrida 1989, vxii). The literary critic and colleague of de Man, Geoffrey Hartman, described his death as a 'tragedy' (Waters and Godzich 1989, 4), while in an essay written shortly after de Man's death the renowned American literary critic J. Hillis Miller asserted that 'the millennium of universal justice and peace among men ... would come if all men and women became good readers in de Man's sense' (Miller 1987, 58). In 1999 the post-colonial, Marxist critic Gayatri Chakravorty Spivak dedicated her book *A Critique of Postcolonial Reason* to Paul de Man, who had died sixteen years earlier. Despite these testimonials, de Man is a controversial figure whose work inspires devotion and denunciation in equal measure. His theoretical work is variously described as 'incomprehensible', 'anti-human' or 'apolitical', while wartime journalism rediscovered shortly after his death has led to de Man being branded a 'Nazi sympathiser' by several of his critics.

However Paul de Man is judged, he is a key figure in the history of

critical thought and in continuing critical debate. His innovative and
meticulous readings illuminate not only literary texts but also questions of language, philosophy, and politics. In fact, much of what is now
taken for granted in literary studies came about as the result of
ground-breaking work by de Man. Perhaps most often associated with
deconstruction, which will be discussed in detail below, de Man was
one of the first generation of literary critics to introduce explicitly
theoretical ideas into literary criticism. From the 1920s to the 1960s,
literary studies in North America and the UK had been dominated by
New Criticism, which thought of itself as a 'common sense' approach
to reading. This type of criticism emphasises the importance of form in
contrast to content, meaning, or context and thinks of the literary text
as a self-contained aesthetic object comprised of formal unities, which
make texts 'great works'. Several New Critics created their own canon
of literary works to exemplify the eternal truths of great literature.
During the 1950s a number of Anglo-American literary critics began
to engage with contemporary European philosophy, finding that they
shared common interests in such questions as language, perception,
and identity. They also began to question conventional ideas about
history and the concept of the human self. They looked to Europe, and
in particular to French intellectual activity during the 1960s and
1970s, as source of inspiration, rather than looking to the Anglo-
American tradition. In this context, then, 'theory' refers to the body of
knowledge that is now called post-structuralism, which develops an
understanding of the literary from certain works of European philosophy and psychoanalysis. The concentration on the canon characteristic
of the New Critics provides a focus for the other dominant strand
within Anglo-American literary criticism, the writing of literary
history.

By 1970 Paul de Man was based at Yale University in America, along
with several other like-minded thinkers now credited with significant
contributions to the 'theoretical turn' in literary studies. These
academics contributed to the development of literary studies through
their individual publications, but also became, as a group, the subject
of furious debate. The interest in post-structuralism generated by the
pioneering work of de Man and others led to considerable friction
within the academic institution. Traditional forms of literary criticism
felt threatened by the radical implications of this new body of knowledge and an often acrimonious debate ensued between old and new, in

a period in Anglo-American intellectual life (roughly from the mid 1970s to the end of the 1980s) which has been dramatically called the 'theory wars'.

It becomes difficult, in fact, to separate de Man's writings from the context of academic in-fighting in which they emerged. As a result, to trace the development of his thought and the varying reactions to his work is in some way to sketch out a history of literary theory in the academic institution. However, any attempt to explain the emergence of 'theory' in terms of a simple chronology would be to adopt a naïve model of history which theory has done much to question. Nevertheless, Paul de Man is significant not only as an important point of reference during the theory wars of the 1970s and 1980s, but as a sensitive reader of Romantic literature and the canon of European philosophy and for the range and complexity of his ideas. He can be thought of as a pivotal figure in the bringing together of American and European thought, having spent his formative years in Belgium but pursuing his academic career in America.

## DE MAN'S CAREER

De Man was born in Antwerp on 6 December 1919. As mentioned above (and discussed in more detail in chapter 6), he spent his formative years in Belgium. He then emigrated to the United States at the age of 27, arriving in New York in 1948. After spending some time as a clerk, freelance critic, and French teacher, he decided to complete his education, which had been interrupted by the war in Belgium. He gained his Ph.D. from Harvard University in 1960 with a thesis entitled 'Mallarmé, Yeats and the Post-Romantic Predicament'. While de Man's work at this time shows an interest in the canon of European philosophy (notably in the work of Martin Heidegger), his critical style seems to follow a cross between perceptive close reading and the dominant contemporary concern with literary history. De Man would later devote much time to criticising the ethical and political implications of this mode of criticism in the posthumous volume *Aesthetic Ideology*. After a successful defence of his doctoral dissertation he moved from Harvard to Cornell, where he stayed until 1969. In the late 1960s he also held a visiting lectureship at the University of Zurich and from 1968 to 1970 he was a Professor of Humanities at Johns Hopkins University in Baltimore. After 1970 de Man made a permanent move to Yale, the institution with which his name is most frequently associated. In 1979 he was made Sterling Professor of Comparative Literature and French, a post he retained until his untimely death.

In terms of publications, de Man's output was relatively modest, some seventy-five essays and reviews written between the award of his doctorate and his death. Most of these essays have subsequently been collected into edited volumes. Only two of these were published in his lifetime, although he planned other collections of previously published essays. De Man's first published collection, *Blindness and Insight: Essays in the Rhetoric of Contemporary Criticism*, appeared in 1971, with a revised edition in 1983. This is a mix of theoretical essays, close readings of literature and philosophical speculations around the theme of then 'contemporary' critical writing. The work includes essays first written between 1955 and 1971. The value of these essays is that they reflect the development of new thought in literary criticism during this period. They range from accounts of Heidegger's reading of German poetry in the 1950s to discussions of a perceived crisis in American New Criticism in the 1960s, concluding with early appreciations of deconstruction at the start of the 1970s. This was followed by *Allegories of Reading* (1979), which explores literature and rhetoric, arguing that the study of literature, providing an insight into the general structures of language and textuality, is fundamentally important to understanding the world in which we live. Some of de Man's most influential essays appear in the first collection to be published after his death, *The Resistance to Theory* (1986). The essay that gives this volume its title helped to define the direction of theoretical inquiry during the so-called theory wars and it is hard to over-emphasise its importance to the growth of literary theory in the English-speaking academy. In this work we see de Man, a member of a generation trained in New Criticism and literary history, encouraged by an encounter with European philosophy in the 1950s and 1960s to open out the unproductive classifications of literary criticism. *The Rhetoric of Romanticism* (1984) expands theories presented in *Allegories of Reading*, confirming the importance of de Man's work on Romantic thought. *Romanticism and Contemporary Criticism* (1993) is in some ways a companion volume to *The Rhetoric of Romanticism*, but gathers a range of essays from 1954 (before de Man began to study literature at university) to 1981. This collection treats de Man's lifelong engagement with the Romantic mind, but also examines the reception of Romanticism in twentieth-century literary criticism. These collections were followed by *Aesthetic Ideology* (1996), which should by rights be thought of as a 'sequel' to *Allegories of Reading*, as the essays included were written between 1977 and 1983. This is a profoundly political account of the relation between rhetoric, the production of knowledge and aesthetics, which flies in the face of frequent accusations that de Man's work is apolitical. It appears that de Man's next project was to focus, in part, on Karl Marx, reaffirming the 'political' direction of his work. Sadly, de Man died before he was able to fully elaborate this project.

## DE MAN AND DECONSTRUCTION

One result of the 'theoretical turn' is the profusion of approaches to reading (the many 'isms' of theory) which inevitably appear in any study of thinkers from de Man's period. As this book continues, such approaches (structuralism, reader-response, etc.) will be explained as necessary, but the one key term to any study of de Man is *deconstruction*. The mature work by de Man contained in *Allegories of Reading*, *The Rhetoric of Romanticism*, *The Resistance to Theory* and *Aesthetic Ideology* cannot be separated from deconstruction and for this reason, in exploring why de Man is important, it is essential that we should examine the concept of deconstruction.

### DECONSTRUCTION

The word 'deconstruction' is most commonly associated with Jacques Derrida (b. 1930), a philosopher at the École des Hautes Études en Science Sociales in Paris, who has also held visiting professorships in various North American universities. Derrida is interested in the ways in which the philosophical, literary, and cultural discourses of the West are constructed through what he calls *logocentrism*, or the repeated gesture of putting *logos* (the Greek term for 'word', more widely translated as 'meaning' or 'sense') at the centre of a text. Derrida's basic criticism of western thinking is that it most commonly operates by privileging certain terms to the exclusion of others, while presenting that exclusion as natural (for example, the privileging of Man over Woman or West over

East). In this way understanding is closed off rather than opened up to the rich possibilities of meaning within a text. However, as Derrida is at pains to point out, there is no easy escape from a logocentric way of thinking because as users of language we cannot help but look for central or stable meanings. A reading of a text that follows this passage of privilege and exclusion, in order to over-turn the hierarchy it implies, and to open the text out to an affirmation of the absence of a fixed and authoritative central meaning, is called a deconstruction.

It is almost impossible to define 'deconstruction'. However, the following points may be useful:

1  Deconstruction is not a method of criticism. The idea of a method presupposes a fixed set of rules to apply to a text. Deconstruction only has one rule: allow the other (what is different, the not-me) to speak.

2  Each example of deconstruction is unique to the context in which it appears. A deconstruction involves placing oneself within a text, following its contours and becoming inextricably bound up in the text. Deconstruction does not critique texts, but reads texts leaving a trace of their moment of reading within them. Deconstruction does not 'do' anything, rather it shows what is already happening within a text.

3  Deconstruction shows the ways in which binary thinking is the logo-centric pattern of western thought, serving particular political interests. A binary opposition is a false hierarchy in which one term is privileged over another marginalised term (e.g. Man/Woman, West/East). To deconstruct a binary one must affirm the importance of the marginalised term, showing the ways in which the privileged term relies on it for its definition, then displace the terms by a way of thinking which does not involve binary logic at all.

4  Deconstruction questions the legitimacy of any closed system of thought. Deconstruction shows that what is assumed to be outside of a system is in fact always already at work inside it, contaminating the purity of the system.

5  Deconstruction takes 'presence' as its theme. Presence is the desire for stable, fixed and unitary meaning, for centres, origins, a God, a point of authoritative meaning. Logocentrism desires presence and

attempts to stabilise meaning by excluding contradictions and inconsistencies. Deconstruction shows that seemingly stable entities are not always as they appear.

6 Deconstruction uncovers the history of concepts. All concepts have a history. If a concept can be shown not to be natural, but to be historical and to be inconsistent within its history, then its privileged (or stable) status may be in doubt.

7 Deconstruction says that 'there is nothing outside the text'. This does not mean that readers should only pay attention to the words on the page or that everything is just an effect of language. Rather, it means that nothing happens outside of an experience of textuality. The text that we read is not divorced or separate from the context in which it appears. Instead, all the contextual concerns of a text (history, politics, biography etc.) are also textual (inextricably bound up in language). In this way there is no getting outside of textuality into a supposed non-textual 'real' world.

8 Deconstruction undoes the binary between 'close readings' and 'contextual readings' which divides the institution of literary criticism. Deconstruction follows the detailed work of language within a text and also opens the text onto its historical, social, and political contexts. 'There is nothing outside the text' also means there is nothing but context.

9 Deconstruction rejects every attempt to set limits or boundaries to meaning. Deconstruction reads philosophy but also literature, architecture, art, film, politics, jurisprudence, and so on (without limit). Deconstruction cannot be assimilated to any existing programme (philosophical, political, cultural) because deconstruction is always already at work within such programmes undoing this very gesture of appropriation (inside/outside). Deconstruction likes mess, contamination, impurity, impropriety.

10 Deconstruction cannot be reduced to the work of Derrida and de Man, or their many readers. Deconstruction is simply the name Derrida gives to what happens in texts (philosophical, literary, cultural, political) regardless of any 'outside' interference by a reader.

Although de Man is now strongly associated with the practice of deconstruction in America, he did not always 'do' deconstruction, as his earlier essays reveal. De Man met Jacques Derrida for the first time at the Johns Hopkins University in Baltimore, at a 1966 conference with the theme of 'The Structuralist Debate'. This conference opened the door in North America to a growing interest in certain French philosophers and theorists. It transpired that Derrida and de Man shared an interest in the work of the Enlightenment philosopher and novelist Jean-Jacques Rousseau and that both were working on Rousseau's lesser-known text 'Essay on the Origins of Language'. However, de Man did not at this time share Derrida's approach to the work. In 1977 de Man wrote a critical appreciation of Derrida's commentary on the text, in his essay 'The Rhetoric of Blindness: Jacques Derrida's Reading of Rousseau' (*BI*, 102–42). This essay will be discussed in more detail in the following chapter, but for now it is worth noting that in this and other early engagements with the term deconstruction, de Man displayed a deep ambivalence towards the concept. And certainly, whatever de Man meant by the term deconstruction as he used it in later texts, was not always reducible to, or identical with, Derrida's use of the term. De Man's story is the story of a certain generation of critics and of the post-war history of literary criticism, but it is also the story of a specific moment in the history of deconstruction.

While teaching on the literary studies program at Yale, de Man taught alongside the critics Geoffrey Hartman, Harold Bloom and J. Hillis Miller. Along with Jacques Derrida who arrived at Yale in 1975 to teach a few weeks a year, this group came to be known – somewhat misleadingly – as the 'Yale School' or the 'Yale school of deconstruction'. The phrase is unfortunate not only because Derrida was not based at Yale, but also because the gathering was not a school (where members of a school share a common methodology and a collective critical project) and not all of them were exponents of deconstruction. While the writings of de Man, Hartman, Miller and Derrida share certain family resemblances, they do not speak with the one voice and never describe themselves as – or attempt to outline – any sort of critical project. Harold Bloom, meanwhile, has been a strong and public critic of deconstruction. This extraordinary collection of fine readers, by accident rather than design, found themselves at Yale during a critical period in the history of Anglo-American literary studies. They provided a focus point for media interest in the dissemination of the charismatic, potentially subversive, undoubtedly foreign, new wave of criticism, which was developing rapidly within the American university system. The appeal of 'The Yale School' to the journalism that had given it its name was already on the wane by the time of de Man's death in 1983, but the period had proved a productive one for the thinkers concerned. It was at this time, as de Man came into proximity with the constant support and exchange provided by Hartman, Miller and Derrida, that he wrote his greatest essays, including those in the 1979 volume *Allegories of Reading*.

A final note should perhaps be added on the label of 'Yale School' or 'American' deconstruction, which is often erroneously described as a form of deconstruction concerned with the close reading of literature and less philosophically engaged than 'French' deconstruction. According to this view 'American' deconstruction is a reinvention of the close-reading style of New Criticism. However, a close examination of de Man's texts and those of his colleagues will reveal that this judgement is highly superficial. In thinking about the term 'American deconstruction' the context of the 1980s 'theory wars' is significant. This widely held idea that de Man, Miller and Hartman's work can be characterised as an aberrant form of deconstruction arises from the conflicts and debates of this time. On the one hand, there appears to be a desire that America should assimilate the foreigner, deconstruction, and produce its own literary version. On the other hand, the phrase also implies a wish to pigeon-hole and so dismiss or trivialise de Man's, and others', work. This may be indicative of an anxiety caused by the challenge that de Man's writing poses for traditional forms of literary criticism. Certainly, those who had a vested interested in traditional forms of criticism reacted strongly to what was thought of as 'a foreign invasion' and treated deconstruction with extreme scepticism. However, it is also true that deconstruction also found a productive intellectual environment in America, particularly among students and a younger generation of academics who saw its radical potential. Finally, this categorisation into 'pure' and 'aberrant' deconstruction imposes the type of division which deconstruction itself would reject. Deconstruction is impure, disruptive, open, hybrid, changing, overdetermined and incomplete, as will become apparent in this study of the work of Paul de Man.

## THIS BOOK

This book will involve a consideration of each of de Man's published volumes. A chapter will be devoted to each text in chronological order, outlining the key concepts within that text and relating them to the general movement of de Man's thought. In this way, the book will build into an overview of de Man's writing and serve as an introduction to what de Man understood by the term 'deconstruction'. In so doing, the book will attempt to disentangle de Man's writing from the misunderstandings that are commonly associated with their reception. These chapters will be followed by an account of the so-called 'de Man affair' in 1987, when it was revealed that de Man, as a young man, had written for the collaborationist press in occupied Belgium during the war. This event deepens our understanding of de Man as a person but does not necessarily change an appreciation of his mature work. Much of the scandal associated with de Man's name is related to this incident, so it is given serious consideration in this study. The book ends with the section 'After de Man', which reflects on the importance and impact of de Man's work for literary studies and the wider field of critical and cultural theory. This is followed by detailed suggestions for further reading, including primary and secondary sources. This book is not a substitute for reading the texts of Paul de Man. It cannot hope to render an absolutely accurate account of de Man's thought because it must by necessity summarise and reduce the complexity of that thought. Rather, this book is a step towards reading the work of this key critical thinker. It will afford you an entrance to the greater complexity and rigour of de Man's texts and show you just how rewarding an engagement with these texts can be.

# KEY IDEAS

# 1

# LITERARY LANGUAGE
# AND MISREADING

## *Blindness and Insight*

Almost everything Paul de Man wrote is related to the question of reading. The primary interest of literary theory and the purpose of critical thinking is that it will make us better readers. However, de Man's understanding of the term 'reading' radically expands the meaning of that term, displacing it from its conventional use. Hillis Miller says of de Man's use of the term, that reading is 'the ground and foundation of the whole of human life' (Miller 1987, 48) because 'reading' for de Man includes not just reading as such, certainly not just the act of reading works of literature, but 'sensation, perception, and therefore every human act whatsoever' (Miller 1987, 58).

*Blindness and Insight: Essays in the Rhetoric of Contemporary Criticism* (1971), de Man's first collection of essays, shows the early development of de Man's understanding of reading and explores related ideas on literary language. The volume also reveals de Man's early engagements with deconstruction with which he is now so strongly associated. This chapter will begin by examining the essay 'Literature and Language: A Commentary' (a text added to the revised edition of *Blindness and Insight* in 1983) which encapsulates de Man's key ideas on the question of reading. In outlining his own definition of reading, de Man identifies the misreading of literary language at the heart of many contemporary critical theories and develops the idea that critics (paradoxically) display the greatest blindness at their moments of greatest insight. The second half of the chapter turns towards de Man's essay 'The Rhetoric of Blindness: Jacques Derrida's reading of Rousseau'. In this essay we see de Man's early ambivalence towards Derrida's deconstruction, but also the development of the ideas which underlie his own later form of deconstruction.

## LITERATURE AND LANGUAGE: A COMMENTARY

'Literature and Language: A Commentary' (1972) was originally published in the journal *New Literary History* as a review of other essays contained in an issue entitled 'The Language of Literature'. The essay is a useful introduction to what de Man means by reading because it comments on the work of his contemporaries, the reader-response theorist Michael Riffaterre, the phenomenological critic Stanley Fish, the structuralist Seymour Chatman, and the humanist critic George Steiner, and so defines the difference between these theoretical positions and de Man's own thought. In a sense this essay contains everything that de Man says about reading in this and later books. This is in spite of the fact that it appears as a second appendix to the main text, and might somehow be considered less important or 'central' to the argument of the book. However, as de Man repeatedly shows in his analysis of literature, the most decisive indication of the concerns of a text are to be found in its margins. If, as de Man argues in later works, there is no authoritative centre in a text, no core of fixed meaning, then there is no single point more important than any other and there can be no 'proper' starting point for reading.

In this essay, de Man's first criticism of the popular understanding of literary language within literary criticism is that while it is easy enough to define a sub-set of literary language such as metaphor or rhyme, it is extremely complicated to define what it is that characterises literary language in general. De Man complains that each of the essays he reviews are too quick to assume that such a definition is possible.

## LITERARY LANGUAGE IS NOT WHAT YOU THINK

In this appendix de Man's criticism of the essays he reads makes a useful check-list of errors to avoid when thinking about literary language. These errors can be associated with particular modes of theory, as indicated below:

1 Don't say 'texts are made up of words, not things or ideas' (New Criticism) because what do words refer to if not ideas and things?

2 Do not assume that we know what 'great literature' is (Humanism). This glorifies literature and makes it inaccessible.

3 Do not say literary language has no relation to ordinary language (Humanism). Do not say literary language is merely ordinary language (Structuralism). Both statements too readily assume that we know what 'ordinary language' is.

4 Do not suppose that a new understanding of language consigns all previous knowledge to the dustbin (Reader-Response). New knowledge is based on a reading of old knowledge.

5 Do not separate a study of literary language from the experience of reading (Phenomenology). This would be to immobilise a text.

6 Do not maintain that literary language is characterised by its fictional status (Linguistics). Not all literature is fictional: think of memoirs and letters.

7 Do not imagine that literary language is produced on the surface of a text by deep structural operations within it (Structuralism). This only extends the metaphor of inside/outside to the body of a text.

8 Do not ignore inconsistencies and aberrations within literary language that unsettle traditional models of rhetoric (Phenomenology, Structuralism, Reader-Response). These will be the points at which such models fall apart.

9 Do not think that a pure study of literary language is possible outside of the misreading and misinterpretation of texts.

In reviewing the similarities and differences between the essays de Man suggests that despite the numerous different theoretical approaches brought into play, the general shape of each essay is the same: they all rely on an opposite theory against which they define their own understanding of literary language. All the essays involve a critical reading of previous, supposedly incorrect, theories of literary language and de Man complains that each of the essays is concerned with what they assume to be a knowable entity, literary language, rather than reflecting on their own status as examples of reading. That is, to the extent that the conflicting positions proposed by each of the essays cannot all be correct, the nature of literary language must be being misread in some, if not in all, of the essays. In this way each essay misreads literature by performing (copying or doubling) a misreading by someone else. For example, if Reader-Response theory gives its own definition of literary language as a development of New Criticism's definition, and this earlier definition is a misreading, then Reader-Response theory will involve a reading of a misreading and so produce another misreading. Thus, a theory of literary language – as it is represented by these essays – cannot be separated from the problem of misreading. This leads de Man to ask how a study of literary language can ever begin if every proposed theory is the result of a misreading. Therefore, in order to address the nature of literary language de Man finds it necessary to reflect on the prior question of what he calls 'misreading'.

In contrast to the essays under review de Man proposes that reading itself is an obstacle to literary understanding and not something merely secondary to the appreciation of literature. In other words, when we try to define literature in terms of the language it uses we are asking the wrong question. Literature is a problem of reading, or more accurately misreading:

> The systematic avoidance of the problem of reading, of the interpretative or hermeneutic moment, is a general symptom shared by all methods of literary analysis, whether they be structural or thematic, formalist or referential, American or European, apolitical or socially committed.

> (*BI* 282)

When de Man refers to reading he does not mean the traditional use of this word as a transparent interpretation of words on the page by a reader who controls meaning through the exercise of his/her will. He is critical of hermeneutics (the branch of literary theory concerned with interpretation) which is content 'to reassure at all costs [more] pragmatically or more formalistically oriented colleagues about the self-evident possibility of achieving correct readings' (*BI* 282–3). For de Man the task of reading is not all straight-forward. The hypothesis of *Blindness and Insight* is that not only does a reading say something the text does not say but it even says something the reader did not mean to say. It is not just that critics unknowingly misinterpret texts but that the very nature of language makes reading impossible.

## RHETORIC

De Man connects the question of literary language to that of misreading. All of the essays under consideration, using different vocabularies, assume that literary language can be categorised according to rhetorical schema.

However, says de Man, the history of Rhetoric as a discipline shows how difficult it is to maintain fixed boundaries between different kinds of rhetorical tropes. For example, when does catachresis (the misuse of a word) become metaphor (the non-literal application of a word); when does metaphor (in which a thing is spoken of as being that which it only resembles) turn into metonymy (in which the name of one thing is put for that of another related to it)? At best the transition from one rhetorical figure to another is fluid. Similarly, the distinction between literary language and ordinary language is difficult to maintain rigorously. When does journalism turn into literature and when do memoirs become literary? The question of what is specific about literary language comes down to the problematic status of rhetoric. De Man suggests that the determining characteristic of literary language is figurality (rhetorical uses of language). In this way rhetoric is to be understood in a wider sense than that implied by the strict codes of figures of speech in traditional literary analysis. For de Man, rhetoric is not a distinct object suitable for literary analysis but is the figurative dimension of language 'which implies the persistent threat of misreading [i.e. the possibility of meanings other than those intended by a speaker]' (*BI* 285) in both so-called 'literary' and so-called 'ordinary' language.

De Man does not accept that readers, or for that matter authors, are in control of meaning. Rather the 'truth value' of an interpretation can never be verified in relation to the text being read because the figural dimension of language – from which no reading can escape – always interferes with the desire to set a fixed meaning to a text. Rhetoric is a use of language that constantly refers to something other than itself. For example, in Sherlock Holmes's metaphorical description of Moriarty as 'the Napoleon of crime', Moriarty is not literally Napoleon but has certain qualities which Napoleon had (leadership, ruthlessness, ambition etc.). Figural language does not suppose a single meaning (Moriarty is Napoleon) but makes reference to a chain of meanings, which has no one authoritative centre. Therefore, because rhetoric by definition does not refer to single and fixed meanings, the interpretation of rhetoric cannot lead to set readings with essential centres.

Just as we read figurative language in the text, our interpretation is also based on figurative language. Criticism is not 'ordinary language' to literature's 'rhetoric'. Rather, our readings are as open to unlimited meaning as the texts we read. Thus, just as there is no absolutely fixed meaning to the text we read, there is no authoritative centre to our reading. Our own readings are always open, fluid and provisional. It is the belief of readers and critics that this is not the case, and that definitive or absolutely true readings are possible, which de Man calls misreading. As soon as we recognise rhetoric at work within a piece of writing, says de Man, its 'readability' is put into question. Readability here refers to the possibility of producing an essential or definitive reading. The moment we acknowledge that such readings are impossible we cannot bring an end to the task of reading. Language as rhetoric makes it impossible to place a limit on meaning in a text and so prevents closure (the fixing of meaning) in that text. This is as true of the text of my reading as it is for the literary text I read. Any reading is therefore open to further interpretation. However, one could not possibly go on reading forever even if one wanted to, and wherever a reading has to stop it is bound to be inadequate. For this reason 'reading' as such (in its traditional sense) is strictly impossible. This might not be welcome news for literary critics and academics who have built their reputations on the strength of supposedly 'definitive' readings. However, for de Man it is a serious prospect and he later writes in *Allegories of Reading* that 'the impossibility of reading should not taken too lightly' (*AR* 245).

## A NEW DEFINITION OF READING

For de Man, then, reading means the interpretation of figurative language. Since there is no clear distinction between figurative language and ordinary language, de Man's definition of reading calls for us to read the world around us. Figurality appears in literature but also in film, art, philosophy, histories, advertising, television, biography, journalism, conversation, and so on. In so far as figurality is characteristic of all language it also determines the way we talk and the way we think. In fact perception itself cannot escape figurality. By 'reading', therefore, de Man means a critical challenge to perception, which refuses to accept a desire for stable or single meanings. Because we are always participants within language and we are continually interpreting and perceiving the world, there can be no end to the task of reading. Certainly, one will never have read enough, or, ever be able to read enough. This, for de Man, is the tragic linguistic predicament of the human condition. It is tragic because, as we have seen, it is not altogether certain that reading itself is possible.

'Literature and Language: A Commentary' presents a radical challenge to the way reading is understood and so challenges the whole discipline of critical interpretation. For this reason some of de Man's critics have accused him of attempting to undermine the traditional values of scholarship in the humanities. Such a rebuke is not necessarily untrue. De Man's work is not merely a matter of stressing the importance of reading to literature, rather it is a complete displacement of all the traditional categories (author, reader, text, literary language, ordinary speech etc.) of literary analysis. Geoffrey Bennington points out that de Man's understanding of the impossibility of reading should not be mistaken for a variety of reader-response theory:

> When Paul de Man claims that 'the systematic avoidance of the problem of reading, of the interpretative or hermeneutic moment, is a general symptom shared by all methods of literary analysis ...', he is inviting anything but the return of the subject and the so-called act of reading.
>
> (Waters and Godzich 1989, 213)

We should not confuse de Man's deconstruction of 'reading' with any simple notion of the reader as a producer of meaning in a text. De Man does not merely privilege the reader over the author as the source of meaning in a text. This would be just an inversion of a binary opposition, which did nothing to displace the self-assured model of reading – characteristic of conventional literary criticism – that produced the binary in the first place. Neither does de Man want to abolish the idea of reading or of literary criticism altogether. On the contrary, what makes de Man's text a deconstruction is its positive affirmation of reading and literary language. It takes these concepts and works them through, rescuing them from the way they are understood by conventional (logocentric) thinking, and proposes an understanding of the terms that displaces that traditional order of thought. It is not that literary criticism is wrong in its thinking about reading but that literary criticism has not thought about reading enough. De Man proposes, to use a familiar turn of phrase in deconstruction, reading without Reading. That is, an understanding of reading which does not rely on the logocentric definition of reading as the discovery of essential meanings. Similarly, the essay also calls for rhetoric without Rhetoric. An understanding of the figurative, free from the fixed idea of rhetoric as a use of language confined to literature.

De Man's short essay, 'Literature and Language', gives us an opening into two of his most important concerns: reading and rhetoric. It also explains the main argument of *Blindness and Insight*, namely, that all critical readings are misreadings. That is to say, all critical texts have, what de Man calls, a 'critical blindness' to their subject matter. For example, he argues that while New Criticism insists that the study of literature should be based on a close attention to language – 'the words on the page' – it is blind to the obvious consequences of this.

New Criticism resists anything like a linguistic vocabulary to describe literary language and has no interest in understanding the phenomenon of language beyond its appearance in literary rhetoric despite demonstrating the importance to understand precisely this. In particular, it identifies literary language as innately ambiguous and paradoxical. If New Criticism where to follow its own insight to its logical conclusion, de Man says, it would see that the question of language as an innately ambiguous and paradoxical phenomenon would have implications beyond literature. Similarly, each of the essays discussed in 'Literature and Language' are blind to the fact that – while trying to define literature through the type of language it uses – they are all engaged in the process of reading. It is reading, says de Man, which in fact comes closer to defining literature rather than its use of language.

## 'THE RHETORIC OF BLINDNESS: JACQUES DERRIDA'S READING OF ROUSSEAU'

In the essay 'The Rhetoric of Blindness: Jacques Derrida's Reading of Rousseau' de Man gives an example of his notion of critical insight and blindness in relation to Derrida's book *Of Grammatology* (1967).

### JACQUES DERRIDA, *OF GRAMMATOLOGY*, TRANS. GAYATRI CHAKRAVORTY SPIVAK

Most of the work that constitutes Derrida's *De la Grammatologie* was published in the years before 1967. However, the publication of its English translation in 1976 caused an earthquake in the American academy. It remains one of the most important philosophical texts of the late twentieth century. Grammatology is the study of writing. Derrida argues that throughout the western philosophical tradition the concept of 'writing' has been subjugated to the more immediate and supposedly prior concern of 'speech'. Western philosophy thinks of writing as derived from, or secondary to, speech. However, this is merely an effect of the desire for presence which seeks to assert the seemingly knowable authenticity of the spoken voice in preference to the problematic absence of (author)ity in a piece of writing. In fact, says Derrida, speech cannot be prior to writing because any kind of speech already presupposes the existence of a linguistic system in which it participates. This linguistic system is based on structural relationships and conventions (grammar) that produce meaningful language. Derrida equates grammar with Writing as a system of inscription, i.e. a general system of signification, which precedes and gives meaning to any individual act of linguistic production, written or spoken. There can be no speech without an understanding of grammar, and so writing, in fact, precedes speech. Here Derrida overturns a classic binary opposition of western philosophy. However, speech is not just another form of writing. Rather, writing involves a fundamental and irreducible uncertainty as part of its essential structure. For example, if I write in a suicide note 'The fact that you are reading this note means I am dead' then the meaning of this sentence is entirely cut off from its author. If this sentence were not readable after my death it would not be a sentence and so while it is not necessary for me to be dead to be read, it is necessary that you are able to read me even if I am dead. Therefore, writing does not rely on a point of origin – such as an author – but on the general possibility of inscription, what Derrida calls 'arche-writing' (a writing without origin) or 'Writing' in the more general sense.

In this essay de Man says that all critics 'seem curiously doomed to say something quite different from what they meant to say' (*BI* 105–6). This has a double effect of generating both blindness and insight at the same time. For example, the insight of the New Critics is their attention to the language used within a text, their blindness is their refusal to acknowledge the consequences of the importance of language. De Man argues that critical blindness follows as a result of critical insight, 'critics' moments of greatest blindness with regard to their own critical assumptions are also the moments at which they achieve their greatest insight' (*BI* 109). This is not merely a psychological aberration on the part of the critic but is, argues de Man, 'inextricably linked to the act of *writing* itself' (*BI* 106, my emphasis). It would seem that de Man is working closely here with the expanded definition of 'Writing' Derrida proposes in *Of Grammatology*. De Man does not mean the act of placing written marks on a page by a conscious agent, but writing in the wider sense of the production of meaning. He goes on to use 'writing' interchangeably with 'reading' as the construction of meaning. In this way de Man's essay enacts its own blindness and insight – its insight being a rigorous critique of Derrida's *Of*

*Grammatology*, its blindness being the unacknowledged use of Derrida's term 'writing' as it is presented in that book.

De Man suggests that the possibility of reading can never be taken for granted because reading is an activity, which can never be observed, prescribed or verified. A text – the inscription of meaning through reading – is not a discrete entity that can be identified in the way that a 'book' can. A book is not a text; a book is merely paper with ink, a text is a construction of sense. It is possible to point to a book, it is not possible to point to a text. For example, both Derrida and de Man read the same book by Rousseau but each reader produces a separate text, i.e. their reading produces different meanings. In 'reading a text' one cannot then appeal to a knowable entity for verification but must remain caught within the reading moment which poses the problem of its intelligibility on its own terms. That is to say, a reading of a text only ever refers to itself (de Man's 'text' is his own reading rather) and not to an observable event (the book which bears Rousseau's name, which has some kind of essential meaning) which can validate its truth or otherwise. De Man states that 'criticism is a metaphor for the act of reading, and this act is itself inexhaustible' (*BI* 107) precisely because it is unverifiable. Thus, any critical insight cannot be validated outside of the terms of the text it reads and any attempt to claim it as a prescribable fact of reading is a blindness to reading's own inexhaustible openness.

In this way critical texts are, for de Man, inherently unstable. They rely on the openness of reading and by necessity attempt to provide a closure to reading in the form of definitive statements. This contradiction leads de Man to propose that interpretation can 'not be scientific' (*BI* 109), meaning that it cannot have a fixed object of study which yields stable and authoritative knowledge:

> Since they are not scientific, critical texts have to be read with the same awareness of ambivalence that is brought to the study of non-critical literary texts, and since the rhetoric of their discourse depends on categorical statements, the discrepancy between meaning and assertion is a constitutive part of their logic.
>
> (*BI* 110)

In other words, critical texts (because they are texts) are no more fixed in their meaning than literary texts, but because they are critical texts they involve making definitive assertions of the stability of their meaning and this inconsistency is what makes a critical text possible. De Man suggests that 'there can be no escape' from this impossible logic and in fact this dilemma is 'the irreducible philosophical problem raised by all forms of literary criticism' (*BI* 110).

So, de Man turns to Derrida because he finds that, unlike the literary critics he reads elsewhere in *Blindness and Insight*, Derrida restores 'the complexities of reading to the dignity of a philosophical question' (*BI* 110). According to De Man, Derrida makes reading integral to the major statements he makes about the nature of language in general. The reason that de Man praises Derrida over the French novelist and critic Maurice Blanchot or the Belgian philosopher Georges Poulet (who also attempt to account for the problem of reading) is that Derrida's notion of reading emerges from specific encounters with individual texts rather than a generalisation about the reading process from a wide-ranging experience of reading, as in the case of Blanchot and Poulet. However, this does not make Derrida's reading free from the *double-bind* of critical blindness and insight. A double-bind is an experience of impossible contradiction to which one cannot help but respond. To de Man, Derrida's 'reading of Rousseau [*Essai sur l'origine des langages*] in *Of Grammatology* can be used as an exemplary case of the interaction between critical blindness and critical insight, no longer in the guise of a semiconscious duplicity but as a necessity dictated and controlled by the very nature of all critical language' (*BI* 111). In this way, de Man subjects Derrida's deconstruction to his own 'pre-deconstructive' method of analysis.

## JEAN-JACQUES ROUSSEAU (1712–1778)

Swiss-born, French-speaking philosopher and novelist of the eighteenth century. His philosophical texts include *On the Origins and Foundations of Inequality* (1754) and *The Social Contract* (1762); literary texts include *Julie, or the New Héloïse* (1761), *Émile* (1762), and his celebrated *Confessions* (1771). Rousseau's writings are synonymous with the period of democratic revolution and 'Enlightenment' from which they emerge. De Man's treatment of Rousseau in 'The Rhetoric of Blindness' can be thought of as a dry run for the second half of *Allegories of Reading* (see chapter 2) in which Rousseau's texts are read as exhibiting a 'deconstructive' knowledge before the fact.

De Man begins his reading of Derrida by suggesting that *Of Grammatology* is little different from the long history of Rousseau criticism, which has, in de Man's opinion, misread him. As in traditional criticism of Rousseau, Derrida identifies a bad faith on Rousseau's part concerning literary language. Rousseau condemns writing as a sinful addiction but relies on literary language to convey this disapproval. However, while conventional readings of Rousseau are content to put this contradiction down to a psychological flaw in the author or use it to dismiss Rousseau's argument as inconsistent, Derrida sees it as part of a wider linguistic problem. Rousseau condemns rhetoric as an aberrant use of language because his own text is part of a western philosophical tradition which defines writing as a form of absence (negativity or non-existence) against speech as a form of presence (authenticity or existence). The meaning of speech is thought to be immediate and transparent because we can trace it back to its source, which is the speaking (existing, present) voice. The meaning of writing is, however, ambiguous or secondary because it is removed from its origin or author who is not physically present when it is read. For this reason, the western tradition of philosophy privileges speech, over writing, as more authentic. This is another way of describing logocentrism (see pp. 5–6). Thus, de Man argues, Derrida cannot dismiss or ignore Rousseau because any contradictions within Rousseau's argument are a consequence of the exemplary nature of his text as part of the western philosophical tradition (of which Derrida is also a part).

Derrida's main theme in *Of Grammatology* is the recurrent repression in western thought of all forms of written language, and their reduction to a mere appendix or supplement to the live presence of the spoken word. For example, Derrida reads the work of the French structural anthropologist Claude Lévi-Strauss in which music and song is valourised over literature, because literature is said to be merely a nostalgic and distant echo of the more primal and immediate song. Rousseau's discussion of the origins of language seems to fall into this pattern with his insistence on voice as the origin of written language. However, carefully following Rousseau's text, Derrida shows that whenever Rousseau posits a point of presence (the voice as the origin of writing) he always appeals to a prior moment of authenticity and so undermines the privileged status of the voice as an origin. Any attempt to trace the written word back to a spoken point of origin leads to a repetition of the distance between meaning and source which characterises the absence of writing. This is as much to say that speech is not the origin of, or more authentic than, writing. However, even though this is the implication of his argument, Rousseau never states this outright. De Man reads this contradiction as a version of critical blindness: 'Rousseau's own texts provide the strongest evidence against his alleged [logocentric] doctrine ... he "knew" in a sense, that his doctrine disguised his insight into something closely resembling its opposite, but he chose to remain blind to this knowledge' (*BI* 116).

De Man's criticism of Derrida – his identification of a moment of blindness in Derrida's text – is that having followed the intricate pattern of assertion, contradiction and disguise in Rousseau's essay (which Derrida characterises as a necessary condition of any writing) he continues to suggest that Rousseau favours the logocentric doctrine over the opposite argument, which the work of his text reveals. Derrida's reading seems to suggest that Rousseau is consciously engaged in his text when arguing for speech as the origin of writing, but somehow passive or unaware when arguing for the opposite. In other words, just as Derrida is suggesting that the meaning of a text does not rely on an authentic point of origin, his criticism of the *Essai* depends on making Rousseau just such an authentic source. Derrida's characterisation of Rousseau is only valid if one suggests that the meaning of his text relies on what Rousseau consciously intended it to mean, even though Derrida's own argument does away with consciousness as an authentic point of origin. However, this seeming contradiction in Derrida's argument is no more a flaw than Rousseau's own inconsistency. Rather, following the logic of blindness and insight, Derrida's critical insight coincides with this moment of blindness. The ambivalent question of Rousseau's conscious or unconscious engagement in his argument shows that on the all-important issue of whether the meaning of a text can be traced back to an authoritative source, categories such as 'absence', 'presence', 'passive', 'active', 'distance' and 'authenticity' fail to function as useful indicators of what is actually happening in the text. Thus, the effectiveness of such terms as universal descriptions is undermined by the ambivalence of language in a text. What is important, says de Man, is not the degree of control Rousseau has over his language but what this language says about itself. That is to say, language is more important than the presence of its author or source – which is precisely Derrida's thesis.

## MISREADING AND DECONSTRUCTION

Importantly in this essay de Man equates the impossible double-bind of 'misreading' with Derrida's 'deconstruction' (*BI* 116) which follows the unresolved contradictions of Rousseau's text:

> Derrida's story of Rousseau getting, as it were, a glimpse of the truth but then going about erasing, conjuring this vision out of existence, while also surreptitiously giving in to it and smuggling it within the precinct he was assigned to protect is undoubtedly a good story.

*(BI* 119)

However, de Man goes further in his own reading of Derrida. De Man alights on two passages in Rousseau's essay which complicate Derrida's reading – significantly for de Man these passages concern the use of rhetoric. The title of the third chapter of the *Essai* is '*Que le premier langage dut être figuré*' ('That the first language had to be figural'). This assertion is a direct contradiction of Derrida's reading of Rousseau as a privileger of the presence of voice over written language. Thus, Derrida has to read this section as a moment of blindness in Rousseau in which Rousseau says the opposite of what he means to say. However, de Man goes on to show that Rousseau makes the notion that all language is figural the explicit premise of his theory of the 'origin' of language and that on this very point Derrida has misread Rousseau. Again, de Man sees in Derrida's text 'the point of maximum blindness' coinciding with 'the area of greatest lucidity' because Rousseau's 'theory of rhetoric and its inevitable consequences' (*BI* 136) is in complete agreement with Derrida's own grammatology. Similarly, we might say that de Man's own insight (his criticism of Derrida) occurs at a moment of blindness. To suggest that Rousseau's discussion of rhetoric – in so far as it is also de Man's understanding of the figurative dimension of language – is compatible with deconstruction is to admit that de Man has no objections to Derrida.

Whether he is aware of it or not, from here to the end of this essay de Man begins to set out his understanding of literature which will come to characterise his avowed deconstruction in later texts, even though he continues to criticise Derrida. Firstly, he notes – following Rousseau – that the term 'literary' in its fullest sense designates 'any text that implicitly or explicitly signifies its own rhetorical mode and prefigures its own misunderstanding as the correlative of its rhetorical nature' (*BI* 136). That is to say, texts are figurative, are aware that they are figurative, and will inevitably be misread as a consequence. Secondly, 'it follows from the rhetorical nature of literary language that the cognitive function resides in the language and not the subject' (*BI* 137). The question for de Man is not whether the author or reader is aware of the contradictions within a text but whether the language of a text is aware of its own inconsistencies. Thirdly, 'the myth of the priority of oral language over written language has always already been demystified by literature, although literature remains persistently open to being misunderstood for doing the opposite' (*BI* 138). In other words, rhetoric (or the literary, in its wider sense of figural uses of language) by its very nature undoes any idea of authenticity or presence in meaning, even if the desire for presence insures that rhetoric will always be misread in this respect. Fourthly, 'there is no need to deconstruct Rousseau' (*BI* 139). De Man argues that Derrida's criticism of Rousseau was not based on a reading of Rousseau's actual essay (which he shows to be in agreement with Derrida's thesis) but on a reading of the tradition of Rousseau criticism which thinks of Rousseau as a defender of speech over writing. For de Man there is no need to deconstruct Rousseau, not because the established tradition of interpreting Rousseau is not 'in dire need of deconstruction' (*BI* 139) but because the text of Rousseau deconstructs itself. This understanding of literature and language will be the subject of the next chapter.

# SUMMARY

In the early collection of essays *Blindness and Insight* de Man outlines an understanding of the term 'reading' that radically expands the meaning of this term. In so doing he outlines some of the concerns that will later characterise his mature use of deconstruction:

- Reading for essential meanings (the traditional approach of literary criticism) is impossible and any attempt to do so will always result in the misreading of a text.
- In so far as a critical reading must attempt to make definitive statements about the meaning of a text, it will always be misreading.
- Rhetoric or figurative language, by definition, makes single, stable or essential meanings impossible.
- However, rhetoric is not a special use of language reserved for literature. All language is figurative.
- It is the nature of critical writing that whenever a critic is most insightful they will also be blind to the implications of that insight.
- Texts, if not authors, are aware of their own insights and blindness and perform this contradiction in their reading.

# 2

# RHETORIC, READING AND DECONSTRUCTION

## *Allegories of Reading*

De Man's second book, *Allegories of Reading: Figural Language in Rousseau, Nietzsche, Rilke, and Proust* (1979), is perhaps his most important contribution to literary studies. It is a book that sets itself up for endless rereading and no summary of its complex architecture can do it justice. However, as a point of entry one might consider the title itself as an extension of themes previously outlined in *Blindness and Insight*. As with the essays discussed in the preceding chapter, *Allegories* is concerned with questions of reading and with a study of figural language (rhetoric or so-called literary language). While many of the essays in *Blindness and Insight* remain fixed within a traditional critical vocabulary, *Allegories* is de Man's breakthrough into an unfettered use of the term deconstruction. The first half of this chapter will consider the general thesis of *Allegories*, the second half will examine de Man's bravura reading of Rousseau's *Confessions*, which closes the book, as a case-study in the work de Man attempts here.

## PHILOSOPHY AND LITERATURE

Despite the intricacy of de Man's close readings the book has large ambitions. His aim is to consider the operation of logocentrism in terms of rhetoric. As we saw in 'Why de Man?', logocentrism is the desire to find fixed and stable meanings at the centre of texts.

However, the stable appearance of such orders is the result of the privileging and exclusion of certain terms within the architecture of a text. The operation of logocentrism in philosophy is called metaphysics. Philosophy is an important topic for deconstruction because our understanding of all of the concepts that define the enterprise of everyday life comes from philosophy. Ideas such as reading, writing, selfhood, politics, justice, the nation, friendship, sexual difference, drugs, truth, and so on, are all philosophical concepts. Far from being a marginal discourse within western culture, philosophy is rather the ordering principle around which western thought is organised. It is important, therefore, if the effects of logocentrism are to be understood that we examine the work of logocentrism in philosophy and philosophy as a system of logocentrism (metaphysics). That is, we interrogate the privileged or marginal status accorded to certain terms within the philosophical tradition.

De Man outlines his project for *Allegories* in the opening essay 'Semiology and Rhetoric'. He notes that the authors considered in the first-half of the book (Rainer Maria Rilke, Marcel Proust, and Friedrich Nietzsche) are concerned with a deconstruction of the rhetorical status of metaphysical concepts, such as the self, history, and knowledge. The writers de Man studies here and elsewhere can be pieced together to form a tradition of the critique of metaphysics which runs from Romanticism into Modernism. The key to this critique, says de Man, 'is the rhetorical model of the trope or, if one prefers to call it that, literature' (*AR* 15). If, as de Man proposes, all language is figural ('the trope is not a derived, marginal or aberrant form of language but the linguistic paradigm par excellence. The figurative structure is not one linguistic mode among others but it characterises language as such' (*AR* 105)) then the language of philosophical concepts is also figural. What interests de Man is the way in which philosophical concepts such as 'friendship' or 'drugs' go unrecognised as concepts, rather presenting themselves as innocent or natural terms. This action is the definition of logocentrism, but de Man suggests it is also a rhetorical gesture. It is tropes or 'literary figures' which, when operating in 'ordinary language', produce the action of logocentrism. For example, the word 'drugs' is a metonym (a part which stands for the whole, e.g. in the phrase 'the crown of Scotland' the word 'crown' is a metonym for the monarch). When we use the term 'drugs' its meaning is determined not by a scientific definition (to science both aspirin and cannabis are drugs) but by ethical and political concerns (responsibility, society, the body etc.) which is a philosophical definition. When we use 'drugs' (the word rather than the thing) it stands metonymically in the place of an entire conceptual order which underpins its meaning.

Therefore, according to de Man, philosophy is figural. This suggestion deconstructs the binary opposition between philosophy and literature, which pervades the tradition of western thought since ancient Greece. Philosophy has always been thought of as having a unique relation to truth, while literature is a form of fiction and so revels in its status as non-truth. In this scenario the non-truth of literature is clearly related to its use of figurative language, which is a form of deception. For example, while a poet may say 'flowers are gold' flowers are not actually gold. Traditionally, this has led to literary and philosophical texts being read in different ways: one as 'serious' and one as 'non-serious'. However, de Man proposes that philosophy uses the same language as literature and is therefore open to the same sort of rhetorical analysis as literature (and should be read in the same way). But as de Man notes in 'The Rhetoric of Blindness' literature, because of its rhetorical nature, deconstructs itself or performs the contradictions which structure it (see p. 28). Therefore, if philosophical texts are equally aware of their rhetorical status they will also deconstruct themselves, demystifying the metaphysical concepts they contain while remaining open to a logocentric misreading that views them as doing the opposite. For de Man 'literature' and 'philosophy' are not separate discourses. Rather 'literature' is de Man's word for the behaviour of tropes (so-called 'literary language') while all texts are 'philosophical' because they produce knowledge. On the one hand, de Man continues to read Literature (poetry, prose, and drama) because such texts provide an abundance of information about rhetoric and so are keys to understanding language in general. On the other hand, he notes that 'if one wants to conserve the term "literature", one should not hesitate to assimilate it with rhetoric, then it would follow that the deconstruction of metaphysics, or "philosophy", is an impossibility to the precise extent that it is "literary"' (pp. 14–19). The deconstruction of metaphysics is said to be impossible because for de Man the 'literary' (the rhetorical, the figurative, or the tropological) always already deconstructs itself.

## ALLEGORY AND NARRATIVE

Chapter 3 of *Allegories* considers a moment of textual self-reflexivity (a point at which a text calls attention to itself as a text) in Marcel Proust's novel *A la recherche du temps perdu*. It concerns a section early on in Proust's novel in which the narrator describes an episode from his childhood when he lies on his bed reading. For de Man this moment is significant because it involves a text making a theme of reading and so calling attention to its own reading. In his understanding of Proust, de Man presents a summary of the argument of *Allegories*. In a nutshell he notes 'any narrative is primarily the allegory of its own reading' (*AR* 76). Of course for de Man this means that any narrative is also the allegory of its own misreading, but what is meant by the term 'allegory'?

## ALLEGORY

*Allegory* is a literary figure in which one thing refers to something else. For example, a dove is an allegory of peace. If we come across an allegory like this in literature we recognise the dove as a bird but we realise that the significance of the dove lies in the fact that it refers to something else.

For de Man all narratives are allegories because – following the logic of *Blindness and Insight* – any reading of a narrative will produce not only something that the narrative does not say but also something that the reader does not mean to say. Therefore, the interpretation of the narrative (in effect its meaning) refers to something other than itself. Since we can have no knowledge of the narrative outside of a reading of it, and this reading will always be a misreading, the narrative (our reading of it) will always refer to something other than itself.

De Man calls this effect of language 'allegory' because it involves a gap between reference (the word or text) and referent (the thing referred to) as in the discrepancy between dove-as-peace and dove-as-dove. For de Man this gap between reference and referent is not confined to narrative but is a general condition of all language (because all language is figural). It is in this gap that miscommunication, misrecognition, and misreading takes place. Any communication might be said to be a miscommunication, and just as de Man's displaced definition of reading calls for a challenge to perception any reading of the world must also be a misreading of the world. However, misreading is not a delusion but a necessary part of meaning. De Man notes that rhetoric 'escapes control of the self' and it is at this point that 'writing' begins (in the sense of Derrida's use of 'Writing' as the general possibility of meaning, see p.27). Meaning relies on misreading. If there were a simple and transparent relation between what I said and what you understood me to say then there would be no need for interpretation, no possibility of multiple meanings in a text, and only one authoritative centre (me) producing a single, stable meaning. We know that this is not the case and that meaning is always plural. However, as we can see, to make such an assertion is not a matter of simply saying that readers create their own meaning or that all readings are equally valid. De Man would not agree with either statement. Rather, if all language is figural it lends itself *structurally* (or by necessity) to misreading and this misreading is a basic condition of producing meaning at all.

For de Man the episode in Proust can be called an 'allegory of reading' for several reasons. Firstly, it is literally an allegory (or representation) of reading, the use of reading as a theme in literature as a way of calling attention to the text's own status as a text and challenging the reader to consider the very process of reading and the experience of textuality. Every narrative, says de Man, tells the story of its own reading. Secondly, it is a demonstration of reading as a question of allegory, or of misreading in which a text always refers to something other than itself. De Man goes on to deconstruct this passage, showing that it relies on incompatible meanings. It is impossible to decide whether one is true and one is false because the text can only be judged on its own terms as a text and not against any outside criteria which would justify a claim of true or false. For example, the narrator describes the kitchen maid as resembling the Renaissance painter Giotto's allegorical fresco 'Charity'. This is an ambiguous description since the literal image rendered in this fresco appears to mean the opposite of 'Charity'. The viewer requires Giotto to literally spell out the meaning of the painting by writing the Greek word '*KARITAS*' in the upper frame. Thus, while the maid may be charitable we could equally read her – after Giotto's image – as unkind. It is impossible to decide which is true and which is false by reference to the text alone or even by reference to the fresco. Thirdly, the knowledge produced by this episode of reading affords us an entrance to a wider scheme of reading as a challenge to perception and to the general conditions of language and textuality. In this way, de Man's critical strategy involves opening up a text (to close reading and onto wider concerns) by making an incision in the text at one key moment. In *Allegories* this cut often takes place – as it does here in de Man's reading of Proust – around an episode of reading or of textual self-reflexivity. Such moments are what de Man calls 'the defective cornerstone of the entire system' (*AI* 104).

While we should be wary of any architectural metaphor which seems to imply that meaning is determined by structure rather than being in a state of flux and radically unpredictable, this paradoxical phrase, 'defective cornerstone', seems to neatly describe the double action of de Man's critical incisions. Like a cornerstone these episodes are seemingly unimportant or marginal, pushed to the side or hidden from view. However, the cornerstone is in fact the most important stone, the one around which all the other stones are placed, the stone which supports the entire house. Yet, this is a 'defective' cornerstone, i.e. one that will cause the house to fall down. Its position is precarious and unstable, ready to fall at the slightest push. The reader would aid the work of the defective cornerstone by exerting leverage against the entirety of the architectonic system. That is to say, the reader follows the work of the text's own deconstruction rather than pushing from the outside. For de Man, every stone is a defective cornerstone.

De Man pursues this consideration of narrative as allegory into his later reading of Rousseau to propose a description of the general work of textuality. He states that a narrative only ever tells the story of its own deconstruction. However, de Man says that while all narratives recount their own impossibility, not all narratives are the same:

> The paradigm of all texts consists of a figure (or a system of figures) and its deconstruction. But since this model cannot be closed off by a final reading, it engenders, in its turn, a supplementary figural superposition which narrates the unreadability of the prior narration. As distinguished from primary deconstructive narratives centred on figures and ultimately always on metaphor, we can call such narratives to the second (or the third) degree *allegories*. Allegorical narratives tell the story of the failure to read whereas tropological narratives, such as [Rousseau's] *Second Discourse*, tell the story of the failure to denominate. The difference is only a difference of degree and the allegory does not erase the figure. Allegories are always allegories of metaphor and, as

> such, they are always allegories of the impossibility of reading – a sentence in
> which the genitive 'of' has itself to be 'read' as a metaphor.
>
> (*AR* 205)

Every text presents a trope and then proceeds to undo, or deconstruct, the presentation of that trope. However, this deconstruction cannot be closed off and so opens the text onto a series of readings and rereadings, none of which can achieve closure (we will see an example of this in a moment when we read Rousseau's *Confessions*). Therefore, says de Man, all narrative always tells of its failure to narrate (i.e. its failure to achieve closure in a definitive telling). Each reading, or retelling, demonstrates the previous reading to be a misreading and thus demonstrates its own status as a misreading. According to de Man, a text like Rousseau's *The Social Contract* – in which he describes the rules of civic society as contract or agreement drawn up between citizens – tells of the inability to read the figure of the contract as a trope (i.e. the failure to see the contract as both concept and metaphor). De Man calls this an 'allegorical narrative' because the text engenders more than one degree of reading within itself, and so what seems like a deconstruction of a central figure also contains within itself the demonstration of the impossibility of the reading that deconstructs the figure in the first place. The discovery that something, which claims to be true, is a mere trope is only the first step in de Man's deconstruction. The second step is to disclose how the corrective impulse within this analysis is obliged to act out a misreading of its own in an attempt to establish it as the true or corrected version. Hence, this sort of narrative points to a reading of its own processes and is allegorical – it refers to that which is not identical with itself (i.e. its own misreading). While some texts (tropological narratives) remain within a pattern of only demonstrating the figural or narrative nature of what de Man calls 'denomination' (the act of stating or naming, rather than telling) the difference between tropological and allegorical narrative is not strict.

De Man's definition of narrative is not confined to literature, as he says of Rousseau's novel *Julie* and the philosophical text *Profession de foi*, 'no distinction can be made between both texts from the point of view of a genre theory based on rhetorical models. The fact that one narrates concepts whereas the other narrates something called characters is irrelevant from a rhetorical perspective' (*AR* 247). In conventional accounts of language, narrative (telling) is opposed to denomination (naming), with the denominative mode privileged as the natural order of language and narrative marginalised as a deviant form found only in fiction. For example, philosophy has been traditionally considered a denominative, rather than narrative, mode – Derrida famously opens his book of memorial essays for de Man with the philosophical rebuke 'I have never known how to tell a story' (Derrida 1989, 3). De Man wants to displace this binary to show that 'all denominative discourse has to be narrative' (*AR* 160). Since any denominative act is figural, it is susceptible to the gap between reference and referent and is therefore open to the possibility of misreading like any narrative. A narrative is a trope and as such is open to the deconstruction of its own figurality, 'a narrative endlessly tells the story of its own denominational aberration and it can only repeat this aberration on various levels of rhetorical complexity' (*AR* 162). A narrative both tells and names (telling the story of Scrooge also names the events of his life), it is – to use some of de Man's favourite terminology – both 'performative' and 'constative' (it *performs* the act of telling a story but also *states* facts, e.g. 'Jacob Marley was dead'). Indeed, telling someone that something happened (narration) can, on occasion, be so close to saying that something is (or was) the case (denomination) that it is impossible to draw any rigorous distinction between these two modes. Or, more generally, it is questionable whether we can draw any absolute distinction between narrative discourse and any other form of verbal behaviour. Since all denomination is a form of telling, any tropological narrative (a narrative which states rather than tells) must also tell of the failure to narrate as well as the failure to denominate (for example, see de Man's reading of *The Social Contract* which follows, p. 39). That is, in other words, its failure to achieve definitive closure in either the act of telling or stating. Thus a tropological narrative must also demonstrate the deconstruction of its own denomination. So, all tropological narratives are allegorical, and any narrative narrates its own failure to narrate.

## TEXT AND GRAMMAR

However, de Man's understanding of textuality is not restricted to rhetoric. He does not simply privilege rhetoric over structure. Rather, he defines a text as:

> The contradictory interface of the grammatical with the figural field. ... We call *text* any entity that can be considered from such a double perspective: as a generative, open-ended, non-referential grammatical system and as a figural system closed off by a transcendental signification that subverts the grammatical code to which the text owes its existence. The 'definition' of the text also states the impossibility of its existence and prefigures the allegorical narratives of this impossibility.
>
> (*AR* 270)

'Grammar', you will recall (see pp. 21–2), refers to the formal elements of a text that contribute to the production of meaning. These are sentence structure (grammar in its limited sense) and also the larger system of language (structural effects beyond the level of the sentence) which the text presupposes in order to give it meaning. This is grammar in Derrida's sense of 'Grammatology'. In this latter sense 'grammar' is the very possibility of meaning and, as a formal field, generates the text without fixing it to a single, stable and authoritative centre. De Man suggests that a text is produced by the incompatible tension between grammar as an open field of meaning and the action of rhetoric which at one and the same time presents a figure as a closed concept and then deconstructs that figure.

For example, Rousseau's *The Social Contract* describes society as a contractual relation between citizens who all agree to act in accordance with the law and goes on to make certain recommendations as to how this contract should be observed. However, de Man argues that Rousseau's own text demonstrates the impossibility of a contract. A contract is a form of promise and the text shows that a promise can only be recognised as a promise when it is broken. If a promise such as 'I promise to be at the cinema tonight' is kept, it is not at all certain that I was promising anything, but that it was pre-ordained and definite that I would always be at the cinema at that time. This does not involve me keeping a promise because I have done nothing I would not have done anyway. To promise to do something that I was already doing, or going to do, is not much of a promise. Only if I do not turn up can we be certain that I was not destined to be at the cinema and so did in fact commit to do something in the form of a promise. *The Social Contract* presents the idea of the promise as what it would like us to understand, while simultaneously demonstrating the impossibility of knowing the promise, and so by this reckoning making the promise the only thing worth knowing.

In this way the figural dimension of language, which puts 'the promise' in play, at once closes off meaning (logocentrism) and undoes the meaning it presents (deconstruction), folding around itself in a (mis)reading of its own misreading. Thus a text like *The Social Contract* is generated when this contradictory gesture comes into conflict with the endlessly open production of meaning in the grammatical field. In other words, all texts presuppose the possibility of their own reading (in terms of a single and fixed meaning) but demonstrate the impossibility of such a reading.

## KEY MOMENTS IN *ALLEGORIES OF READING*

Another way of thinking about de Man's notion of rhetoric is to say that 'literalism' (believing words to be the literal truth) is to mistake language (which is innately figurative) for reality. For example, literalism is the belief that by saying the word 'table' I am engaging with a real thing rather than using a word, which is only a metaphor for the thing described by 'table'. De Man argues that 'literalism' is not the absolute truth but rather an effect of language. The literal cannot exist outside of rhetoric. De Man provides us with two important examples of how the relation between rhetoric and the literal works. The first is an analysis of Rousseau's discussion of the word 'giant' (*AR* 149–54) the second describes rhetoric itself through the metaphor of a key (*AR* 173).

In the 'Essay on the Origin of Language' Rousseau writes, 'A primitive man, on meeting other men, will first have experienced fright. His fear will make him see these men as larger and stronger than himself; he will give them the name giants.' Later the primitive man realises that the others are not larger than he is and so invents the word 'man' to describe them while retaining the term 'giant' to describe the object he had previously feared. De Man suggests that this is how literalism works. The word 'giant' does not describe an outer characteristic of the men but rather refers to the primitive's own interior feeling of fear. To say 'giant' is simply to say 'I am afraid'. This fear is not derived from observable facts (the men are not large) but from the primitive's own inner distrust at meeting a new animal. Fear is the result of the discrepancy between outer appearance and inner feelings: the men do not appear hostile but they may be hostile. This hypothesis can never be proven or disproven by empirical data but must remain for the primitive as a permanent possibility. The term 'giant' is a metaphor because it relates the interior feeling of fear to outward properties of size. It may be an error but it is not a lie; the men are not larger but the primitive is afraid. Thus the word presents as certain what is only a possibility, it turns hypothesis into fact (the literal truth). De Man concludes, 'this is an error, although it can be said that no language would be possible without this error'.

In the second example de Man warns against confusing his displaced notion of rhetoric with its traditional use, which views rhetoric as the tool of the individual. Conventionally 'rhetoric' is associated with persuasion, eloquence and manipulation. This is in contrast to a supposedly 'literal' use of language that prevents such deviousness on the part of an individual. In this understanding of rhetoric it acts as a key to understanding the individual (both the manipulated and the manipulator). However, rhetoric seems to be so effective that de Man suggests: 'One may well begin to wonder whether the lock [the individual] shapes the key [rhetoric] or whether it is not the other way round, that a lock (and a secret room behind it) had to be invented in order to give a function to the key. For what could be more distressing than a bunch of highly refined keys just lying around without corresponding locks worthy of being opened?' In other words, *it is not the individual who shapes rhetoric but rhetoric which produces the individual*. In fact, the idea of 'the individual' is a rhetorical trope, which will both describe the experience of individuality and deconstruct that experience.

## CONFESSIONS

The concluding chapter of *Allegories* provides us with an exemplary deconstruction, which demonstrates all of the concerns discussed above. It is a reading of two passages in Rousseau: the first is the conclusion of book II of the *Confessions* (1771), the second comes from the fourth reverie in *The Reveries of a Solitary Walker* written some seven years later. Both passages concern the same episode from Rousseau's youth. The first three books of Rousseau's *Confessions* recount embarrassing or shameful moments in his childhood and adolescence. The reader is encouraged to believe that they are the first person to whom Rousseau has revealed these incidents and 'that the desire to free myself, so to speak, from this weight has greatly contributed to my resolve to write my confessions' (*AR* 278, de Man's translation). However, the episode of Marion and the ribbon so haunts Rousseau that he returns to it in his later text.

While employed as a steward in an aristocratic household in Turin, Rousseau stole a 'pink and silver coloured ribbon' (*AR* 279). When the theft is revealed Rousseau blames a young maidservant, Marion, for having given him the ribbon and by implication suggests that she did so in order to seduce him. When confronted publicly Rousseau sticks to his story, thus irreparably damaging the girl's good name. Rousseau in fact has a crush on the maidservant. However, although Marion has never done Rousseau the slightest harm he destroys her reputation for morality and honesty. She is so sweet natured that she does not protest against Rousseau's public denunciation of her or offer her own counter allegation. Rather she says, 'Ah Rousseau! I took you to be a man of good character. You are making me very unhappy but I would hate to change places with you' (*AR* 279). Both Rousseau and Marion are dismissed and while Rousseau goes on to become a best-selling novelist, his confession speculates at length on the terrible things which are bound to have happened to Marion in her subsequent life.

De Man states that 'to confess is to overcome guilt and shame in the name of truth' (*AR* 279). A successful confession should aim only to provide a true account of events regardless of the light in which this puts the confessor, and by confessing receive forgiveness for one's shameful behaviour. However, in the *Confessions* Rousseau is not content to state the facts of the case: 'It could certainly never be said that I tried to conceal the blackness of my crime' (*AR* 280). He also finds it necessary to offer an excuse for his actions – 'I would not fulfil the purpose of this book if I did not reveal my inner sentiments as well' (*AR* 280) – and so undoes the work of his confession. In explaining why he acted as he did Rousseau risks absolving himself from blame. Since his confession is not a practical act of reparation but exists only as a verbal utterance, de Man asks, how do we know if we are dealing with a *true* confession? Since Rousseau's recognition of his guilt as part of his confession implies the exoneration of that guilt in the name of the same principle of forgiveness through truth that allowed for the certainty of Rousseau's guilt in the first place? In this way Rousseau's confession is said to deconstruct itself.

Rousseau's insistence on expressing his 'inner sentiments' opens up a gap in his discourse. On the one hand, he says that his confession is true and can be verified against knowable facts (the existence of Marion, his dismissal etc.); on the other hand, he introduces into his confession interior thoughts that cannot possibly be verified as true against any outside criteria. We must take Rousseau's word for it that they are true but we can never be certain: while we can verify the truth of the crime we cannot verify the truth of the excuse. Thus, Rousseau's excuse makes plain the unreliability of his confession, which had only been a suspicion until then. Rousseau's text cannot provide closure to his act of confession, modulating from confessional into apologetic mode. Any confession – because it seeks forgiveness – involves a process of exoneration and the failure to confess is always already present within the excuse. Hence, Rousseau's confession demonstrates the impossibility of a true (or pure) confession and confesses its inability to confess. This failure to achieve closure in confession leads to the expansion of the confession and its repetition in the *Reveries*.

For de Man the ribbon represents another moment of textual self-reflexivity. He suggests that its movement between the characters in the narrative can be read as an exchange of meaning, 'once it is removed from its legitimate owner, the ribbon, being in itself devoid of meaning and function, can circulate symbolically as a pure signifier [unit of meaning] and become the articulating hinge in a chain of exchanges and possessions' (*AR* 283). As the ribbon changes hands, from its rightful owner to Rousseau to public revelation and allegedly from Marion to Rousseau, its movement traces, what de Man calls, 'a circuit leading to the exposure of a hidden, censored desire' (*AR* 283). This desire is Rousseau's desire for Marion. When Rousseau says 'it was my intention to give her the ribbon' (*AR* 283), according to de Man, he reveals that his desire to possess the ribbon is a desire to possess Marion. Thus, the ribbon itself is a trope and metonymically stands for Marion. It can also be read as a figure of the circulation of desire between Marion and Rousseau but because this desire is not reciprocal and illegitimate the ribbon has to be stolen. The ribbon is then caught up in a chain of substitutions, 'I accused Marion of having done what I wanted to do and of having given me the ribbon because it was my intention to give it to her' (*AR* 284). This episode is an allegory of reading because it reveals a truth about language in general. If we read the ribbon as a unit of meaning and its exchange as the exchange of language then this incident suggests that all meaning is caught up in a chain of substitutions and is constantly deferred. This is another way of describing the phenomenon of misreading. One misreading substitutes for another without ever being able to close off an endless chain of misreading and so any 'true' or perfect reading is constantly deferred. If we take 'reading' in its widest sense to mean any encounter with language we can see that all meaning (as a form of misreading) is constantly deferred in a limitless chain of misreadings.

De Man takes his analysis of the ribbon further. Following Sigmund Freud's psychoanalytic understanding of desire (in which a desire that cannot be openly expressed will be displaced from the true object of desire onto a substitute) de Man proposes that Rousseau's desire is not so much a desire for Marion but a desire to expose his hitherto secret love for Marion. In other words, Rousseau wanted to get caught so that his desire for Marion could be expressed openly. The shame he feels in his confession is not shame at his desire for Marion but shame at his desire to have that desire exposed. In another chain of substitutions one desire stands for another. What Rousseau really wants, says de Man, is neither the ribbon nor Marion but the public scene of exposure which he in fact achieves. The worse the crime, the worse the lie and slander, the better for Rousseau, whose scene of exposure will be all the greater as a result. De Man argues that the more there is to expose the more there is to be ashamed of and so the scene of exposure becomes more satisfying for Rousseau who can then make a belated revelation in his *Confessions* of his inability to reveal. This implies, says de Man, that Marion therefore was ruined not for the sake of the young Rousseau saving face or for the sake of his desire for her but to provide Rousseau with a public scene in which to perform his shame. In other words, Marion's life was ruined so that Rousseau might have a dramatic conclusion to book II of his *Confessions*. This, for de Man, is the most shameful thing about the whole incident.

## EXCUSES

This episode is an allegory of reading because the confessional mode is a model for all writing. Rousseau notes in conclusion to his reporting of this event in the *Confessions*:

> If this crime can be redeemed, as I hope it may, it must be by the many misfor-
> tunes that have darkened the later part of my life, by forty years of upright and

> honourable behaviour under difficult circumstances. Poor Marion finds so
> many avengers in this world that, no matter how considerably I have offended
> her, I have little fear that I will carry this guilt with me. This is all I have to say
> on this matter. May I be allowed never to mention it again.
>
> (*AR* 288, n. 10)

However, he returns to this incident again less than a decade later. His account of the matter in the *Reveries* is not so much concerned with the shame of stealing the ribbon as with the shame of having written about it in the *Confessions*. De Man suggests that this shifts Rousseau's discourse from the reporting of guilt into the guilt of reporting. By extension (de Man is prone to read from the specific to the general) all writing involves an experience of guilt. Reflecting on the lie he told about Marion, Rousseau states 'to lie without intent and without harm to oneself or to others is not to lie: it is not a lie but a fiction' (*AR* 291). This introduction of the question of fiction into another confession once again opens up a crack in a discourse that relies on an idea of absolute truth. If a lie is, under certain circumstances, only a fiction then how can we ever verify the truth or otherwise of these confessions? This is particularly problematic since Rousseau goes on to say that one should not reproach oneself for writing fiction and so manages to exonerate himself for a second time.

This second account of the ribbon is also an allegory of reading. The disruption of fiction within Rousseau's second confession is suggestive of the gap between reference and referent within all language. Fiction is a use of language in which reference (say the story of Scrooge) does not have any relation to an actual referent (a real-life person called Ebeneezer Scrooge). However, such a gap between reference and referent is, as we have seen, characteristic of all meaning as a form of misreading. Thus fiction, for de Man, is not a deviant use of language found only in literature but is the general model of language, in so far as all language involves a suspended relation between what is said and what is understood. However, it is equally the case that it is impossible to isolate a precise moment in Rousseau's texts that might be identified as a fiction. It is importantly undecideable whether it is a fiction or not. De Man suggests that the very moment a fiction is posited it will immediately be misinterpreted as true. This is not only the case in a confession but is true of all language. Language, for de Man, is only ever the presentation of tropes which, through the action of logocentrism, are misinterpreted as being literally true. Again, this misinterpretation is not necessarily an illusion but the general condition of meaning. De Man proposes that without this undecideable moment (which can never be identified) 'no such thing as a text is conceivable' (*AR* 293). Rousseau's confession exists both as an actual event and as a 'fictional' account and it is impossible to decide – because we only ever know about the event through the fictional account – which one of the two possibilities is the correct one. All texts involve such moments of undecideability.

This indecision allows the text to excuse Rousseau's crime as a possible fiction. Conversely, this arbitrary exoneration of dreadful deeds makes fiction the most cruel of activities. As de Man suggests, 'excuses not only accuse but they carry out the verdict implicit in their accusation' (*AR* 293). By excusing himself Rousseau calls attention to his crime and so reaffirms his guilt. For de Man this circuit of accusation, excuse, and guilt goes beyond the conscious intentions of Rousseau as an author. Rousseau may very well wish to confess but his text is incapable of confession. Writing always involves cutting meaning off from its authorial source and so dispossesses the author of meaning, which is instead generated by the text itself. Therefore, says de Man, it is not altogether certain that the excuse exists as a result of a prior guilt but rather the text itself generates the guilt in order to make the excuse contained within it meaningful. Excuses always produce the guilt they exonerate but it is always an excess of guilt (Rousseau's text cannot provide closure to the guilt he feels). Rousseau's text is caught in a contradictory position. On the one hand, no excuse can ever hope to catch up with the production of guilt in a text. On the other hand, any guilt (including the guilty pleasure of writing) can be excused as the product of textual excess. This leads de Man to his final allegory of reading. Since guilt is a matter of cognition (something knowable) and an excuse is a question of linguistic performance, de Man proposes that any linguistic act always produces an excess of knowledge about itself but can never hope to know how it has been produced, which is the only thing worth knowing. In other words, reading as a form of knowledge can never hope to know how readings are produced, even though from de Man's point of view this is the only thing worth understanding.

# SUMMARY

The only full-length study of rhetoric and reading published during de Man's lifetime, *Allegories of Reading*, allows us to think about his unique strategy for deconstruction:

- The language of philosophy is figural and so philosophy (and by extension all seemingly 'factual' discourses) should be read according to an understanding of rhetoric.
- Literalism (the confusion between reality and the words that describe it) is only one rhetorical mode among many. However, no language would be possible without this confusion.
- All narratives are allegories of their own (mis)reading; every narrative tells the story of its own deconstruction.
- A narrative is allegorical because it always refers to something other than itself. This deferral of meaning is characteristic of all language.
- Language lends itself *structurally* to misreading and this misreading is a necessary condition of producing any meaning.
- Every text presents a trope and then proceeds to deconstruct that trope. However, this deconstruction cannot be closed off and so opens the text onto a series of readings and rereadings, none of which can achieve closure.
- Texts are produced at the meeting point between the contradictory actions of language, as an open-ended system of meaning, and rhetoric, which seeks a closed meaning only to demonstrate the impossibility of closure.
- De Man's deconstruction involves opening up a text at a moment of thematic or conceptual contradiction, working through this indecision until the text undoes its own logic.

# 3

# DECONSTRUCTION AS AN EXPERIENCE OF THE IMPOSSIBLE

## The Resistance to Theory

The remaining books in the de Man corpus are all collections of essays edited by others and published after his death. Sometimes these collections follow a selection outlined in de Man's own notes, sometimes they do not. This guide will concentrate on key individual essays, chosen for their particular importance in terms of de Man's contribution to literary studies. This chapter will examine two pieces from the collection entitled *The Resistance to Theory*: the 1982 essay which gives the collection its name and 'The Task of the Translator', a transcript of a lecture given in 1983. In 'Force of Law: the Mystical Foundation of Authority', Jacques Derrida writes that 'deconstruction is the experience of the impossible' (Derrida 1992, 15). The two essays to be examined here reveal the importance of this idea for the work of Paul de Man. They also represent some of most de Man's most influential work, marking the period after the publication of *Allegories of Reading* when de Man's fame and critical powers were both at their highest point.

## 'THE RESISTANCE TO THEORY'

It is hard to over-estimate the importance of the essay 'The Resistance to Theory' to the growth of literary theory in the English-speaking academy. At the time it was written what might be characterised as localised fighting was beginning to turn into the full-blown 'theory war'. In this context the title of de Man's essay was both provocative and timely. The influence of the essay can be measured when we consider that although its content was thought radical at the time much of what de Man says here has now become standard academic opinion. The essay was commissioned by the Committee on Research Activities of the Modern Languages Association for its volume *Introduction to Scholarship in Modern Languages and Literature* as the section on literary theory, athough it was not published here after it was judged unsuitable for the collection – de Man never questioned this decision. The Committee may not have been impressed by de Man's argument in the essay that 'the main theoretical interest of literary theory consists in the impossibility of its definition' (*RT* 3). With this as its key argument, the essay might easily have been entitled 'The Resistance to Deconstruction'.

The title of de Man's essay seems challenging, hinting at the debates raging around deconstruction in the North-American academy at the time, with a note of rebuke for those in reactionary positions. As discussed earlier, traditional literary studies was at this time mounting a rear guard action against what it perceived as a 'foreign invasion' by theories that threatened all the fundamental assumptions of the discipline. The 'traditionalists', if you will, were a strange alliance of conventional scholars (literary historians, literary biographers, New Critics) and some Marxist or materialist critics. Both the New Critics and the Marxists felt something like deconstruction would undermine the core assumptions of their critical enterprise, such as the self-containment of a text or the stability of history. As we have seen this was a justified, if misplaced, fear. But in fact de Man's argument concerns the inherent inability of 'literary theory' to accomplish its own work. The argument is brilliantly spun through a series of substitutions, which involve de Man redefining the phrase 'the resistance to theory' each time.

## THE RESISTANCE TO LANGUAGE

He begins in a literal way with the institutional rejection of theory as an approach to the discipline of literary studies. He defines literary theory as an approach to texts which 'is no longer based on non-linguistic, that is to say historical and aesthetic considerations' (*RT* 7).

Bearing in mind that de Man is contrasting theory to literary history, we might still be suspicious that he is working with a definition of theory which more accurately describes his own work than the heterogeneous discipline we now call Literary Theory (psychoanalysis, post-colonialism, Feminism, Marxism etc.). However, this slippage is understandable given that literary theory was in its infancy at this time.

Contrary to a firmly held opinion of many philosophers, de Man insists that 'the present-day development of literary theory is [not] a by-product of larger philosophical speculations' (*RT* 8). Literary Theory may ask similar questions to philosophy – such as the nature of language or the meaning of art – but it does so in a context freed from the fixed categories adhered to by the philosophical tradition. 'It is therefore not surprising', says de Man, 'that contemporary literary theory came into being from outside of philosophy and sometimes in conscious rebellion to the weight of its tradition' (*RT* 8). Philosophy is not so much a problem for literary theory, as theory is now a concern for philosophy. The non-traditional and innovative thinking of literary theory 'adds a subversive element of unpredictability' (*RT* 8) to the conventional modes of thought favoured by much philosophy and so challenges the way we think about questions such as literature, aesthetics, language, writing, and so on.

Literary theory is defined by de Man as an 'introduction of linguistic terminology in the metalanguage [a language or technical vocabulary used to describe an aspect of language] about literature' (*RT* 8). By this de Man means that literary theory is interested in literature in reference to itself (in its own right) rather than as a way of referring to a 'real world' beyond the text. Rather than saying that literature represents the real world and texts have value because they tell us something about that world, literary theory is concerned with the internal processes of literature itself. This is not to deny the importance of a supposed 'outside world' but to break with a traditional model of criticism which thought of literature as a transparent copy of the world (this act of copying is sometimes called mimesis). This conventional way of understanding literature is supported by an idea of language which proposes that language has meaning as a result of the natural and intuitive use of words by humans to describe their world. In contrast, literary theory thinks of meaning as a function of language itself rather than an act of human will. Theory rejects an Adamic idea of language, in which Adam names the beasts and is the master of language. Instead, theory recognises that the human subject is born into a social use of language, which is already in place, and which s/he learns to use in order to understand pre-existing meanings. For example, as children we do not choose our own names or our cultures. The resistance to theory is, for de Man, 'a resistance to the use of language about language' (*RT* 12), a resistance to talking about language in a different way from the classical schema of philosophy and criticism.

Literary theory, in short, questions all the traditional categories that language and literature have been subordinate to in their disciplinary study but which are not in themselves linguistic or literary. For example, de Man suggests that literature itself undoes all the aesthetic classifications drawn up by philosophy and traditional literary criticism. This is to use the term 'aesthetics' in its strict sense, as it appears in the history of philosophy, as the idea that a work of art can be intuitively perceived by the human senses to be beautiful or not. However, to follow the understanding of textuality proposed by de Man in *Allegories of Reading*, if the meaning of a text is produced by itself, how can its meaning be a matter of intuitive perception by a reader or spectator who imposes their own values on it? Thus, says de Man, 'whereas we have traditionally been accustomed to reading literature by analogy with the plastic arts and with music [i.e. in terms of aesthetic categories], we now have to recognise the necessity of a non-perceptual, linguistic moment in painting and music, and learn to *read* pictures rather than to *imagine* meaning' (*RT* 10). Meaning, for de Man, is always a matter of the processes of language being misread by a reader rather than any allegedly common sense reception of a straightforward use of language. While this latter attitude is on the wane in literary studies, under the influence of de Man's work, it remains the dominant critical mode in the study of music and painting.

De Man points out that if literary theory rejects a mimetic model of literature and the aesthetic categories of art it is not out of a desire to replace them with a purely linguistic understanding of the world. One would understand nothing of deconstruction and de Man's work if one thought of it as merely an extension of the so-called 'linguistic paradigm' (the idealist belief that reality is merely a linguistic construct). Rather, de Man wants to free the study of literature from naïve oppositions between texts and 'the real world' and from uncritical conceptions of art. Literary theory does not deny the relation between literature and the real world but suggests that it is not necessarily certain that language works in accordance with the principles of the supposed 'real world'. Therefore, it is not at all certain that texts are reliable sources of information about anything other than their own uses of language. De Man suggests that to confuse the processes of language with the real world (see pp. 40–1, literalism) is the classic gesture of ideology. In this way, de Man uses this essay to put down the roots of his understanding of ideology which will be the topic of his final work posthumously published as *Aesthetic Ideology* (see pp. 81–97).

However, 'the resistance to theory' is not just a matter of entrenched conservative positions within the institution of literary studies. Rather, says de Man, 'literary theory is itself overdetermined [having too many determining factors to be easily resolved] by complications inherent in its very project' (*RT* 12). If the project of literary theory has been, since structuralism, to found a science of literature then there may be an internal resistance within literature to the very idea of a science, with its strict rules of observation, classification, and prediction.

## STRUCTURALISM

*Structuralism* is the name given to the early, usually French-based, theoretical project (roughly from the mid 1950s to the end of the 1960s) which attempted to found a scientific approach to reading. The usual reading practice of structuralism is to analyse a text in terms of its structure (the overall network of relations between units within a text, structure accounts for the relations between parts and each other as well as parts and the whole). However, the primary insight of structuralism is to suggest that human experience is only possible through the individual's place within systems of meaning, such as language. *Post-structuralism* develops structuralism's understanding of language and the individual, while being critical of structuralism's methodologies and ambition. Unlike post-structuralism, structuralism tends to think of meaning in texts as fixed, which allows it to identify and classify formal structures.

We should remember at this point that 'literature' for de Man is not just a canon of texts but his preferred word to describe the figurative dimension of language (see pp. 17–19). Therefore, the term 'literary theory' refers not only to a theoretical approach to literary texts but also to a theory of the figurative or rhetorical. Given all that de Man suggests about tropes, it almost goes without saying that 'Theory' itself is a trope and that its use in a text, such as de Man's essay, will deconstruct all the meanings that operate under the name 'Theory'. In particular, a theoretical text will surely undo its own pretensions to be theoretical (or scientific) and so theorise its own inability to be theoretical. However, de Man recognises that this is not a sufficient reason to avoid literary theory, anymore than Rousseau's failure to confess was a reason for him not to attempt his confession.

In other words, theory's own internal resistance to the idea of theory is a result of the instability and unpredictability of the figurative dimension of language. Literature, for de Man, is 'the use of language that foregrounds the rhetorical over the grammatical and the logical function' (*RT* 14). This action, we can recall, leads to both the importance of reading and the inevitability of misreading. If literature deconstructs itself, how can a theory of literature help but deconstruct itself as well? The resistance to the idea of theory which emerges within the texts of theory comes about as the result of a conflict between 'theory' as a self-deconstructive trope and the demands of grammar as a system of meaning in those texts. This conflict is brought out in the experience of reading, the process which necessarily involves both. Thus, the resistance to theory is, for de Man, a resistance to reading. The failure to recognise resistance within theory and the failure to account for theory as a form of resistance is, for de Man, a matter of misreading. This misreading can be most clearly seen in those discourses that call themselves theories of reading but which never interrogate the idea of 'reading' on which they depend. De Man is probably thinking of reader-response theory here, which (as we saw in chapter 1) asks us to consider the reader as primary producer of meaning while continuing to think of reading as a straight-forward mediation between a text and an individual. Such 'theories' naïvely believe a science of reading to be possible, based as they are on a traditional understanding of both 'science' and 'reading'.

## THE INSIGHTS OF LITERARY THEORY

In an important passage de Man reminds us of what it means when we talk of reading as a problem for literary theory:

> To stress the by no means self-evident necessity of reading implies at least two things. First of all, it implies that literature is not a transparent message in which it can be taken for granted that the distinction between the message and the means of communication is clearly established. Second, and more problematically, it implies that the grammatical decoding of a text leaves a residue of indetermination that has to be, but cannot be, resolved by grammatical means, however extensively conceived.
>
> *(RT 15)*

That is to say, firstly, that it is impossible – not just 'difficult' but *impossible* – to distinguish between the meaning of a text and the way that meaning is presented in a text (and deconstructed by that text). This is what is meant by the notion of meaning as a function of the text itself, rather than an individual author or reader. Secondly, and consequently, de Man is saying that reading always produces an excess of uncertainty that cannot be understood by the process of reading itself. Reading is *never* a matter of resolving the meaning of a text, it is always a matter of the challenge of *undecideability* posed by meaning, where undecideability expresses itself. Undecideability is the experience of being unable to come to a decision when faced with two or more contradictory meanings or interpretations. It is not the same as 'indeterminacy', a word that suggests a decision has been made and this decision is that a decision cannot be reached. In contrast undecideability stresses the active and interminable challenge of being unable to decide. In this sense, meaning is *radically* independent of the reader, if we conceive of 'the reader' in its traditional sense as a conscious individual exerting their will on a text.

## THEORY AS RESISTANCE

From here de Man goes on to propose that the resistance to theory 'is a resistance to the rhetorical or tropological dimension of language' (*RT* 17) itself. On each occasion that de Man defines and redefines 'the resistance to theory' we must remember that this phrase is working on at least two levels: its literal sense of the resistance to the innovations of literary theory within the academic institution, and its more figurative sense of theory as a resistance to itself. In the case of the former, the resistance to theory is a resistance to the troubling insights which come with a recognition of the effects of rhetoric (in preference, say, to a resolute adherence to literalism in varieties of historical, materialist, or biographical modes of criticism). In the case of the latter, tropes themselves work through a resistance to their own figural status. For example, as discussed in the previous chapter, Rousseau proposes the idea of the contract as a metaphor for society and his text goes on to show the impossibility of the contract. However, a necessary part of this work of self-deconstruction involves the contract as a trope stubbornly sticking to its pretence not to be a trope. It goes unnoticed as a trope, resisting its own figural status. So much so that Rousseau insists on making recommendations for how the contract should be observed. This, once again, is the quintessential action of logocentrism.

Similarly, theory may be just another trope and all theoretical texts must involve a deconstruction of the trope 'theory'. Thus, theoretical texts, by necessity, must always fail to be rigorously theoretical. However, the efficiency of the theoretical enterprise requires that 'theory' itself should not be recognised as a trope and for the theoretical text to present itself as closed. The project of theory necessarily involves a resistance to the recognition of its own rhetorical status. We can identify here a standard gesture in de Man's work: any text (be it a contract, promise, confession, narrative, interview, autobiography etc.) is always, for de Man, about its inability to complete its own project. The text will present its generic theme (the contract, the promise, the confession etc.) and insist on fulfilling its aim (as a contract, promise confession etc.) just as it shows this generic theme to be impossible. This is what de Man means in his opening remarks when he says 'the main theoretical interest of literary theory consists in the impossibility of its definition'. Theoretical texts, like all texts, perform the deconstruction of the central trope which structures them.

It is perhaps surprising then that in conclusion to this essay de Man seems to suggest that 'a "truly" rhetorical reading that would stay clear of any undue phenomenalization or of any undue grammatical or performative codification of the text ... is not necessarily impossible and [is something] for which the aims and methods of literary theory should certainly strive' (*RT* 19). That is, a reading which neither lapsed back into an appeal to intuitive aesthetic categories nor attempted to provide a final resolution to the meaning of a text. However, to propose that 'technically correct rhetorical readings' are possible – de Man's reading of Rousseau's *Confessions* would be a good example – is not the same thing as saying that a 'pure' rhetorical reading would not also be a misreading. In fact, de Man suggests that such rhetorical readings are deeply problematic. Given that they are themselves texts, these readings cannot be verified against any outside criteria which would testify to their truth or otherwise. Thus, on their own terms, these readings are irrefutable. De Man says that they are 'potentially totalitarian', meaning that they offer themselves as potentially closed readings without a set of criteria against which they can be challenged. To say, for example, that Rousseau's confession is definitely true because we know that the theft of the ribbon really happened, is to miss the point that: (a) Rousseau's confession, as a confession, is never anything other than a text, and (b) to confuse knowledge of the theft (i.e. something textual) with the actual theft is to repeat the mistake of literalism. Thus, rhetorical readings do not recognise the terms of a critique like this and are, on one level, seemingly irrefutable.

The structures and functions they expose (contracts, confessions etc.) do not lead us to direct knowledge of language itself but rather suspend any knowledge about language in the form of a text. Textuality being the very thing which prevents intimate contact with language and which stops language as a directly experienced entity from entering into knowledge. Just as a text about a house is not a direct contact with the house but is what in fact prevents the house from being experienced immediately – to think that we experienced the house directly through language would be an error of literalism – so texts about language do not allow for a direct experience of language. Such texts are, in de Man's words, 'consistently defective models of language's inability to be a model of language' (*RT* 19) ). If, as de Man says, literary theory is essentially a way of talking about language then the texts of literary theory must always fail to talk about language. Thus, these texts 'are theory and not theory at the same time' – just as Rousseau's text is at once a confession and fails to be a confession – which points to the only truly 'total' theory, 'the universal theory of the impossibility of theory' (*RT* 19). Hence, any theoretical text that attempts to fulfil its own theoretical project – as any such text must – will result in misreading. So, literary theory cannot help avoiding the very reading it advocates. In fact, says de Man, 'nothing can overcome the resistance to theory since theory is itself this resistance', i.e. if the resistance to theory is a resistance to reading then such a resistance is always already present in theory's own misreading. If theory always fails, 'the loftier the aims and the better the methods of literary theory,

the less possible it becomes' (*RT* 19). This is not a reason to forsake
theory — theory loses nothing in admitting its own impossibility —
rather it is a productive way of thinking about the limits and conditions
of theoretical knowledge.

## 'THE RESISTANCE TO THEORY' AND CHAINS OF MEANING

This essay is characteristic of a common pattern in de Man's thinking.
It works through a series of substitutions in which the term 'the resistance to theory' stands in what is called 'a metonymic chain of
reference' i.e. its meaning is transformed as the argument is pieced
together. In this respect the phrase 'the resistance to theory' is analogous to the ribbon in de Man's reading of Rousseau.

'The Resistance to Theory' is:

1    A resistance to a metalanguage about literature. Therefore it is,
2    A resistance to reading. Therefore it is,
3    A resistance to tropes. Therefore it is,
4    Theory itself. Therefore it is,
5    A resistance to a metalanguage about literature…

De Man uses this structure frequently because it is the pattern
suggested by the linguistic phenomenon he investigates. That is to say,
meaning works by a chain of substitutions. One misreading engenders
another, which engenders another and so on to infinity. The 'true'
meaning of a text is constantly deferred along the metonymic chain.
The point is not that there is a 'true' meaning, which we just cannot
get to, waiting at the end, but that meaning is always in the middle,
always suspended, constantly deferred. The appearance that we have
already reached the end is an effect of logocentrism. Meaning is not
absolute or finite but is never-ending, caught within the perpetual
frontiers of misreading.

## 'THE TASK OF THE TRANSLATOR'

De Man's essay on Walter Benjamin's text 'The Task of the Translator'
appears in *The Resistance to Theory* under the title, 'Conclusions: Walter
Benjamin's "The Task of the Translator"'. The term 'conclusions' is

potentially misleading here. It does not refer to a summation of the views expressed in *The Resistance to Theory* (two other texts follow it in the book) nor does it offer us any definitive conclusions about Benjamin's essay. Rather, this text is a transcript of the last lecture he gave in a series of six at Cornell University in March 1983 (not the finished essay de Man intended for publication but the transcription of a tape recording supplemented by eight pages of rough manuscript notes). These lectures have now been gathered together as the book *Aesthetic Ideology*. Perhaps this essay should be more properly thought of as part of that book, demonstrating the often arbitrary nature of the collected material which now makes up the de Manian corpus. Accordingly the aspects of this essay which deal with the question of materialism will be deferred until the later discussion of *Aesthetic Ideology* in the final chapter of this guide (see pp. 81–97]. In this chapter, the essay will be examined as another allegory of the impossibility of reading.

## WALTER BENJAMIN (1892–1940)

German literary critic and philosopher who earned his living as a literary journalist during the inter-war years. His work responds to the changes in lived existence caused by urbanisation and technology and the varieties of art which come with it. He is often associated with the Frankfurt School of cultural criticism (Max Weber, Theodor Adorno, Max Horkheimer) and his thinking is marked by a pronounced emphasis on the relation of art to history and politics. His writing is also informed by the Jewish tradition of knowledge in which he was trained.

'The Task of the Translator' is Benjamin's introduction to his own translation (1923) of the French modernist poet Charles Baudelaire's (1821–67) *Tableaux parisiens*. It is one of Benjamin's most famous essays (and also one of his shortest and most accessible). As de Man jokes, 'in the profession you are nobody unless you have said something about this text'. The essay argues that translation is strictly impossible. It opens with the assertion that in the appreciation of a work of art a consideration of the reader/receiver is pointless because texts do not transmit information but rather posits the existence and nature of humanity. Therefore, thinking of translation as something to help readers in another language is a red herring. This is what 'bad' translation does. On the contrary, 'translation is a mode' of reading always already present in the original text: 'translatability is an essential quality of certain works' (Benjamin 1992, 71). A translation comes not from the life of a text but from its afterlife. Once a text has been canonised (designated as great literature) and its survival for later generations secured, then its translatability is certain.

Even though it is the task of translation to be as close to the original work as possible, a translation which attempts a literal rendering of a text will always miss the point of the original (its poetic, elusive qualities) and so be a bad or 'unreadable' translation. Paradoxically, a translation must capture the spirit of the original in terms of its own language and thus stray from the literal meaning of the original. In this way, any strict idea of translation is impossible. Translation transforms the language of the translator. For example, a translation of Benjamin's text into English must make English speak German – capturing the subtleties of Benjamin's German prose in English – rather than transposing German into the patterns of English sentence structure. Translation is a 'provisional way of coming to terms with the foreignness of language' (Benjamin 1992, 75), the effects of translation on the translator's own language demonstrating that one's own language is always the most foreign of all. One is always most lost and ill at ease in the language through which we choose to mediate experience, since reality and language never match exactly.

De Man's essay sets out to show that not only is translation impossible (therefore making translation characteristic of reading or meaning in general) but that translation of Benjamin's own text is also impossible. To this end much of the essay is taken up with detailed readings of Harry Zohn's English translation and Maurice de Gandillac's French translation of Benjamin. De Man points out the ways in which these translations fail to capture the sense of Benjamin's German, failing to do so in accordance with principles formulated by Benjamin in his essay. While doing this de Man draws out the implications of Benjamin's essay for a general understanding of language. To accomplish this de Man takes his reader through Benjamin's text in more or less chronological order. This is a frequent gesture in deconstruction. De Man's reading transforms Benjamin's text by imitating its every move, following its contours – even sharing its name – imbricating itself within the text and leaving a trace of itself in what it reads, contaminating the strict division between text and reading. In this way, de Man's deconstruction does not do anything on its own. Rather, it only performs what is already said by Benjamin's essay. De Man does not take Benjamin's essay apart, instead by following its movement so closely de Man's text is able to reveal how Benjamin's essay works. The proximity of de Man to Benjamin allows de Man to come up against the moments of tension and obscure knots of resistance in Benjamin, where the meaning of his text is concentrated.

## THE FAILURE OF THE TRANSLATOR

De Man wants to 'ask the simplest, the most naïve, the most literal of possible questions in relation to Benjamin's text ... what does Benjamin say? What does he say, in the most immediate sense possible?' (*RT* 79). He asks this because Benjamin himself asks 'what does a literary work "say"?' (Benjamin 1992, 70) and answers that it does not 'say' anything in the sense that the function of literature is not to impart information. Hence, a translation which believes itself to be transmitting information into another language for the benefit of mono-linguistic readers is a bad translation because it concentrates on something inessential to literature. De Man also asks this question as a way of introducing the errors of Benjamin's translators (Zohn and de Gandillac), thus showing that it is not necessarily a straight-forward matter to suppose that all literate people can immediately understand and agree upon the meaning of a text. De Man offers several examples of translation errors from each version, but one will demonstrate the point sufficiently. When Benjamin writes in German that 'where the text pertains directly, without mediation, to the realm of truth and of dogma, it is, without further ado, translatable' (*übersetzbar schlechthin*), de Gandillac translates this last word into French as '*intraduisible*' (untranslatable) thus completely altering the meaning of the sentence. Such errors, de Man argues, are not the result of lapses in scholarship by the translators – both translations are excellent renditions of Benjamin's text – rather they are a consequence of the necessary impossibility of translation which Benjamin identifies.

De Man suggests that 'the translator, per definition, fails' (*RT* 80). Any translation is always secondary to the original text and the translation cannot hope to do the same things as the original. In this way the translator has already 'lost' before s/he begins. In German Benjamin's text is called '*Die Aufgabe des Übersetzers*'. '*Aufgabe*' means both task and 'the one who gives up' (a cyclist who gives up in the Tour de France is said to be '*aufgabe*'). Thus, Benjamin's essay could be translated as 'The Defeat [or Failure] of the Translator'. In other words, the translator fails in the task of transposing the original text and translation itself is always impossible. In this sense the translator is unlike the poet or artist who renders the original work. De Man asks, why is this figure of failure exemplary for Benjamin? The answer is that while the poet has some relation to meaning which is not purely within the realm of language (e.g. a naïve relation to a biographical experience), the failure of the translator is a consequence of a purely linguistic predicament. Translation for Benjamin 'ultimately serves the purpose of expressing the central reciprocal relationship between languages' (Benjamin 1992, 73). Thus the translator is caught up in a problem between languages in which questions of desire or intention in meaning are entirely absent because the translator is not the originator of the text.

Benjamin suggests that if translation is unlike poetry it more closely resembles philosophy or literary criticism. This is important for de Man who by extension suggests that translation more readily resembles theories of literature than literature itself. Benjamin also proposes that translation is like history. Philosophy comments on perception but is unlike perception because it is a critical examination of the claims made by perception. Literary criticism or theory derives from literature and would not be possible without the literature that precedes it. History is a result of actions which necessarily precede it. All of these activities are secondary to the original events they describe and are therefore, like translation, inconclusive and failed from the start because they are derivative. However, this derivation is not a matter of copying or imitation (mimesis). It is not a natural or organic process, the translation does not resemble the original in the way that a child resembles his/her parents, nor is it a paraphrase of the original. De Man suggests that for this reason we might say that a translation is not a metaphor of the original (metaphor being the general figure of resemblance, whereby one thing is likened to another). However, the German word for translation, '*Übersetzen*', also means metaphor. '*Übersetzen*' perfectly translates the Greek word '*metaphorein*', to move over or put across. Yet Benjamin and de Man insist that translations are not metaphors (because there is no necessary resemblance between an original and a translation) even though Benjamin's preferred word, '*Übersetzen*', means metaphor. This leaves them with the paradoxical formulation, a metaphor is not a metaphor. It is not difficult to see why translators have difficulties!

The relation between a translation and the original is not one of resemblance or copy, rather the translation relates to what in the original belongs specifically to language and not meaning as a form of paraphrase or imitation. In this way, de Man suggests, that the translation 'disarticulates' the original. That is to say, the translation undoes all the tropes and rhetorical operations of the original, and so demonstrates that the original has always already been falling apart. The failure of translation, which seemed to be a result of its secondary or derived status, is in fact the result of a basic failure of language in the original text. If, as de Man argues in *Allegories of Reading*, all texts perform their own failure then the original text must fail to perform its own translatability. Benjamin had argued that if translation was a mode 'translatability must be an essential feature of certain works'. Thus, in a rewriting of Benjamin's idea of translation as the afterlife of great texts, de Man proposes that translations 'kill the original, by discovering that the original was already dead' (*RT* 84). In this way translations perform a decanonisation of the great work which was already there in the original (unsettling its claim to be an elite text by making it more widely available).

De Man recognises that Benjamin's understanding of translation 'has little to do with the empirical act of translating, as all of us practice it on a daily basis' (*RT* 84). We might call this daily practice of translation logocentric because for purposes of economy, to avoid lengthy explanation and repetition, it suppresses the problematic which Benjamin identifies. This problem has profound consequences for de Man. If translation disarticulates the original to the extent that the process of translation is only concerned with a relation between languages rather than content or information, then translation is always in danger of being sucked into – what Benjamin calls – 'the bottomless depths of language'. Translation always threatens to fall into an abyss of language without end, in which language only ever refers to itself. This discomfort is experienced in not only the language of the original but the language of the translator as well. While we may feel at home in our own language, translation reveals that this language is also disarticulated (falling apart) and always threatening to stumble into the 'essentially destructive' (*RT* 84) abyss of 'pure language' that is always present as a possibility in language. In this way our own language imposes upon us an experience of unease and disconnectedness from which it is impossible to escape. For de Man the human condition is always a matter of an acute linguistic suffering.

## SUMMARY

The collection of late essays by de Man, *The Resistance to Theory*, suggests a particular strategy for deconstruction:

- The essay 'The Resistance to Theory' works through a series of substitutions in which the term 'the resistance to theory' transforms its meaning as the argument is pieced together. This pattern is suggestive of the work of reading itself, which is always caught in the middle of a chain of deferred meaning.
- The essay 'The Task of the Translator' transforms the text it reads by imitating its every move, imbricating itself within it and leaving a trace of itself in what it reads. It does not do anything on its own; rather it merely performs what is already said by the text it reads. It does not take this essay apart, instead its proximity to the essay reveals the moments of tension in which the meaning of his text is concentrated.
- These essays concern deconstruction as an experience of the impossible. The conditions under which 'literary theory' or 'translation' would be possible are the conditions of their own impossibility.

# 4

# DISFIGURATION, DEFACEMENT AND AUTOBIOGRAPHY

## The Rhetoric of Romanticism

Of the two collections containing de Man's essays on Romantic literature (the Rousseau section in *Allegories of Reading* might be thought of
as a third) *Romanticism and Contemporary Criticism* came out later (1993)
even though it is comprised of earlier essays. This volume includes the
Gauss Seminar on 'Romanticism and Contemporary Criticism' given at
Princeton University in 1967 (the same time that de Man was finding
his feet using the term deconstruction, see 'The Rhetoric of
Temporality' included in *Blindness and Insight*). These essays are of
importance in gauging the historical development of de Man's thought
as he negotiates a path from the vocabulary of the traditional literary
criticism, which he found unsatisfactory, towards his more mature
consideration of topics such as allegory, irony, history, and so on. De
Man has a particular fascination with poetry in these essays, which are
not complete and do not seem to have been intended for publication. If
literature is a privileged site for the study of tropes then surely poetry
is the most literary (tropological) site in literature? The essays in *The
Rhetoric of Romanticism* (1984) also focus on poetry. This volume was
edited before his death by de Man himself and, as he states in the
preface, 'represents the bulk of what I have written on Romanticism'
(*RR* vii). As a collection of previously published essays the book is not a
general investigation into Romanticism (as a period of intense historical development for rhetoric) but is a series of examples of rhetoric at

work within Romantic poetry. Accordingly, this chapter will deal with specifics rather than expound something like 'de Man's theory of Romanticism'. The first half of the chapter deals with the essay 'Shelley Disfigured' in which de Man discusses the ways in which a text both produces figures (rhetoric) and disfigures (undoes) them. The second half of the chapter looks at the essay 'Autobiography as De-Facement' in which de Man suggests that the autobiographical mode is character-istic of all writing.

## 'SHELLEY DISFIGURED'

The essay 'Shelley Disfigured' was first published as de Man's contribu-tion to the book of Yale School essays *Deconstruction and Criticism* (1979). At times this essay tends more towards criticism than decon-struction as de Man follows the play of the figures of light and shape in Percy Shelley's poem 'The Triumph of Life' (1822). However, it is the use that de Man makes of this literary device, as a way of thinking about reading literature in general, which could be said to divert his argument from a traditional mode of criticism into something recog-nisable as a deconstruction.

### PERCY BYSSHE SHELLEY (1792–1822)

Second generation Romantic poet noted for his radical political opinions, who scandalised most of European society with his unconventional lifestyle. Married to Mary Wollstonecraft Shelley, author of *Frankenstein*, (1797–1851). Other works include: 'Prometheus Unbound', 'The Mask of Anarchy', 'Adonais', 'Ozymandias', 'England in 1819', 'Ode to the West Wind', and 'To a Sky-Lark'.

What we have of 'The Triumph of Life' tells of a dream-like encounter between the lyric 'I' of the poem and a procession of figures from intellectual and literary history. 'Triumph' in its antiquated sense also means a pageant that celebrates the outcome of a battle. This proces-sion involves characters, such as the English poet William Wordsworth, who were once idealistic in their political outlook but who, after the experience of the seeming failure of the French Revolution and rise of Napoleon, developed reactionary political views. It also includes others such as the philosophers François-Marie Arouet de Voltaire (1694–1778) and Immanuel Kant (1724–1804) whose ideas inspired Enlightenment politics, which later descended into war with American claims for independence and the rise of Napoleon in Europe. The Enlightenment is the name given to the spirit of science, knowledge, and democracy based upon reason (rather than religion) which emerged in the eighteenth century from the work of European philosophy. However, the procession also involves 'the sacred few who could not tame/Their spirits to the conquerors'. Among these is Rousseau (de Man's interest in the poem becomes immediately apparent) who leaves the tableau to converse with the poet. Rousseau explains the meaning of the procession and so guides the viewer through several generations of intellectual history. The thematic concern of the poem is why good intentions dissolve into impure actions, 'why God made irreconcilable/Good and the means of good', in order that Shelley's generation of thinkers might learn from the mistakes of the past.

The poem is unfinished (what literary scholarship calls a fragment) and the 544 lines already in existence were published from the notes Shelley was working on before he was killed in a boating accident in Switzerland. Therefore, says de Man, the poem calls for an archaeological labour of unearthing, editing, and reconstructing. The text itself is structured around the repetition of a series of questions by the poet-observer which mimics this archaeological task – ' "Whence camest thou?/How did thy course begin," I said, "and why?" '. These are the same questions that a reader of the poem must ask about this fragment, 'What is the meaning of *The Triumph of Life*, of Shelley, and of romanticism? What shape does it have, how did its course begin and why?' (*RR* 94). The question of the question is not inconsequential here. De Man suggests that it is the very process of questioning which designates 'The Triumph of Life' a fragment rather than the text itself (which, if we had no knowledge of the biographical circumstances surrounding its production, could well stand on its own as a complete text). It is questions such as these that define the reader's relation to the text, allowing the reader to reconstruct the fragment and so implicitly complete it through their own interpretative act.

De Man likens the work of Shelley to a statue which, having been frozen rigid, is broken or mutilated. The metaphor of the statue is an apt one because it allows de Man to discuss the ways in which so-called 'great literature' (the canon) is monumentalised. Great works (Shakespeare for example) are put upon a peda-stool (to continue the metaphor) to be admired and to be held up as examples of great work. Correspondingly, these texts as statues/monuments are remote and stiff (inflexible in their interpretation). Deconstruction would always want to disfigure such statues, not to pull them down or break them up but to question their canonical status and the working of the canon in general. In the previous chapter we saw that de Man found translation exemplary precisely because it 'decanonised' the original text. 'The Triumph of Life' is also explicitly concerned with the questioning of antecedents in the procession by the poet-observer and by Rousseau.

De Man states that 'the structure of the text is not one of question and answer, but of a question whose meaning, as a question, is effaced [erased] from the moment it is asked' (*RR* 98). The answer to each of the poet's questions is another question, which leads his enquiry down a chain of questions ever further from his original query: 'Whence camest thou?/How did thy course begin ... and why?' De Man proposes that the poem does not give any of the sense of progression that might be expected from a procession of historical characters. Rather, the poem ties itself in syntactical knots as it fails to make progress, effacing and forgetting its own past. One such instance is the confusion and complication of images of light and shape that unfold towards the end of Rousseau's speech. This pattern runs through the poem but one example will demonstrate the point:

A shape of light, which with one hand did fling
Dew on the earth, as if she were the Dawn
Whose invisible rain forever seemed to sing

A silver music on the mossy lawn,
And still before her on the dusky grass
Iris her many coloured scarf had drawn.

(II. 352–7)

Here the run-on lines and lack of punctuation render a single interpretation impossible. On the one hand, the light and water combine to produce 'a silver music' of oblivion. On the other hand, in a not necessarily complementary action, 'and still', they combine to create a rainbow, Iris 'many coloured scarf'. The same syntactical ambiguity, then, generates both an image of erasure and an image of construction.

A detailed reading of this ambiguity throughout the whole poem leads de Man to make a number of important statements concerning two related terms: figuration (the power of texts to posit their own meanings) and disfiguration (the internal structure of a text that erases such meanings).

## DISFIGURATION

De Man suggests that erasure or effacement as a textual ploy is literally a loss of face. Interestingly in French the word '*figure*' can mean 'form or shape' as well as 'face'. The dream-like quality of the experience narrated by the poet involves the blurring of characters' features as they come in and out of view. Such effacement is matched, says de Man, by the erasure of the poet's questioning and the text's (as a self-deconstructive experience) own self-effacement. It is significant then that the principle character of Shelley's drama is Rousseau, whose texts de Man views in *Allegories of Reading* as examples of deconstruction before the fact. The poem becomes so entangled in the erasure of its own questions that de Man suggests that for the poet it is not a case of forgetting a previous condition – because the line between forgotten and remembered becomes totally blurred – but rather as a result of forgetting one can no longer be sure that the forgotten ever existed. What is forgotten is absent just as the poem is involved in the process of forgetting, which cannot in itself make the forgotten present. Thus, the poem articulates a disarticulation and is shaped by the undoing of shapes which – for readers familiar with de Man's critical strategy – resembles the experience of trying to read Shelley's elusive text as well as the experience of reading in general. De Man proposes that the ghostly wavering of characters and figures in the poem is suggestive of a 'near-miraculous suspension' and 'hovering motion which may well be the mode of being of all figures' (*RR* 109). The meaning of a figure (or trope) is neither fully absent nor fully present in its textual manifestation. Its meaning is more spectral: tropes haunt texts.

De Man says of figuration that while it is 'the element in language that allows for the re-iteration of meaning by substitution' (think of the ribbon in Rousseau's *Confessions*, see pp. 41–4), the 'particular seduction of the figure' is not necessarily that it creates an illusion of aesthetic pleasure when reading a literary text 'but that it creates an illusion of meaning' (*RR* 114–5). However, the key to understanding the radical nature of figuration, says de Man, is not to imagine that, say, the figure of light in Shelley's poem is merely the articulation of a natural entity but that the figure 'is posited by an arbitrary act of language' (*RR* 116). For example, the sun is a figure traditionally privileged in poetry as central to poetic concerns about love, life, health, and so on (William Shakespeare's 'Sonnet 130', John Donne's 'The Sun Rising', and Andrew Marvell's 'To His Coy Mistress' spring to mind), while the imagery of stars or night is associated with a different range of meanings less celebrated by poetry. In the natural universe the sun is not any more important than stars (the sun after all is a star, and both give light) rather we impose 'the authority of sense and of meaning' (*RR* 117) on tropes arbitrarily generated by such texts. De Man calls 'the positing power of language' arbitrary because it cannot be reduced to necessity (the natural universe does not have to be like this) but it is also 'inexorable' (unrelenting) because there is no alternative to it for users of language. It is difficult to avoid privileging the sun, even though it is only a trope, when all our metaphors for love and life come from comparisons with it: sunny disposition, sunny side, a place in the sun, etc.

However, this situation leads to a paradox that should warn us against any simple idea that de Man proposes a purely linguistic understanding of experience to the error of literalism (see pp. 40–1). On the one hand, texts posit their own meaning 'and language means (since it articulates)'. On the other hand, language cannot possibly posit its own meaning since meaning is imposed on the arbitrary production of texts by readers who take them actually to refer to something (e.g. the positive value of the sun). In this way texts only reiterate or reflect the errors imposed upon them. For example, the poet in 'The Triumph of Life' shapes the meaning of the procession he sees by the questions he asks about it. However, de Man points out that this is an irresolvable problem (the knowledge of its impossibility makes it no less impossible) because we cannot 'ask why it is that we, as subjects, choose to impose meaning, since we are ourselves defined by this very question' (*RR* 118). The moment we ask a question we presuppose an answer and so are already imposing sense on the language we use. Asking a question closes off alternative ways of thinking and reiterates the structure of meaning we are attempting to interrogate. In this way, de Man says, 'to question is to forget' (*RR* 118) because it erases the arbitrary nature of language in favour of the referential view of language which presupposes that a question will always produce sense (an answer). There is no easy escape from logo-centricism.

This repetitive effacement 'by which language performs the erasure of its own positions' de Man calls 'disfiguration' (RR 119). Disfiguration is a forgetting of the trope as a trope. Language is bound to forget this process of forgetting in order to produce meaning, even though – as de Man points out – knowledge of disfiguration 'is itself a figure in its own right and, as such, bound to repeat the disfiguration of metaphor' (RR 120). Language cannot catch itself forgetting its rhetorical status because such a moment of self-awareness necessarily involves another procedure of forgetting. The process is endless. The nineteenth-century German philosopher Friedrich Nietzsche famously described metaphors effaced by the everyday use of language as 'coins which have lost their pictures and now matter only as metal, no longer as coins' (Nietzsche 1980, 47). This wearing away of faces on a coin as a metaphor for dead metaphors (metaphors which are no longer recognised as such, e.g. 'as sick as a parrot') is almost certainly what de Man is thinking of when he uses the term 'disfigured' here. The trope, like the coin, is forgotten as such because it has been worn away (literally 'de-faced') and circulates not as a trope (coin) but as a literal term (base metal).

However, de Man notes that while the text produces this knowledge of disfiguration (and so to some extent is protected from disfiguration by this self-reflexive 'negative knowledge') it cannot avoid another more literal disfiguration which has come to shape the meaning of the poem, namely, the disfiguration of Shelley's own body in the boating accident in which he died. De Man suggests, 'the defaced body is present in the margin of the last manuscript page and has become an inseparable part of the poem' (RR 120). Hence, the figuration of the poem is interrupted by a disfiguration that determines the meaning of the text although it is neither represented in the poem nor articulated as part of the poem's own meaning. Far from being 'a freak of chance' that the poem is moulded by an actual event, de Man suggests that 'this mutilated textual model [i.e. the fragment] exposes the wound of a fracture hidden in all texts' (RR 120).

Without Shelley to finish the poem for us the task of disfiguration devolves to the reader. The ultimate test of reading 'The Triumph of Life' is then, what do we do with the disfigured body of Shelley, which watches over this text? In a sense the body of Shelley is buried in this text. The poem becomes a monument to the poet. De Man suggests that this is what happens in all canonical texts, they are 'made into statues for the benefit of future archaeologists' (*RR* 121). The so-called great works of literature – like Shelley's final poem – are transformed by their reading into historical and aesthetic objects. This is not neces- sarily a naïve or negative gesture. Shelley himself monumentalises (or buries) Rousseau in 'The Triumph of Life'. De Man states that 'it certainly is not a gesture that anyone can pretend to avoid making' (*RR* 121). If to read is to understand, it is also to question but it is therefore also to forget, to erase and to deface. This defacement (disfiguration) is unavoidable because to question is the very way of life for the user of language: 'no degree of knowledge can ever stop this madness, for it is the madness of words' (*RR* 122). The reader cannot avoid this strategy of questioning because they are a product of it rather than its producer (asking questions presupposes sensible answers which merely repro- duces our own 'working knowledge' of language as referential). Therefore, monumentalisation should not be regarded as either a virtue or defect of a text (good texts are worthy of it, bad texts not) rather, it is a process of reintegrating the arbitrary power of events (biographical or linguistic) back into a logocentric pattern of reading 'regardless of the exposure of the fallacy' (*RR* 122). While 'it is true and unavoidable that any reading is a monumentalisation of sorts' (*RR* 123) the way Shelley disfigures Rousseau in his poem indicates that reading can also allow us to deface the monument. Disfiguration (we could substitute 'deconstruction' here) is a way of resisting any simple notion of literary history as the procession of great names (like the 'triumph' of life). In this way, it proves to be the most historically accurate of approaches because it defaces the idea of history as a monu- ment and as a trope.

## 'AUTOBIOGRAPHY AS DE-FACEMENT'

'Defacement' is then a self-reflexive moment in a text when language both presents a figure or trope and begins to undo (disfigure) it. This dynamic of presentation and erasure (self-deconstruction) is worn away by habitual reading practices (like Nietzsche's coins), and becomes defaced in the text (or more accurately is always already defaced in the text) and passes as a referential use of language. De Man gives a demonstration of this action in his essay 'Autobiography as Defacement', written in the same year as 'Shelley Disfigured'. The deconstruction at work in this essay is once again a response to a singular situation, this time a reading of William Wordsworth's critical text *Essays upon Epitaphs*. Wordsworth's most significant contribution to the genre of autobiography is the poem 'The Prelude' (1798–1839), which de Man makes repeated reference to in this essay. Thus, the *Essays upon Epitaphs* (which were first published as a 'footnote' to the poem 'The Excursion') may seem a marginal place from which to analyse Wordsworth's relation to autobiography. However, in reading these essays de Man is offering a version of the deconstructive strategy outlined in chapter 1, whereby the margins of a text (or body of texts such as the complete works of William Wordsworth) are said to be indicative of the key concerns which structure the entire text.

## WILLIAM WORDSWORTH (1770–1850)

First generation Romantic poet who with Samuel Taylor Coleridge (1772–1834) wrote *The Lyrical Ballads*, a manifesto for Romanticism in English. After spells in Germany and revolutionary France he settled in the English Lake District to dedicate himself to philosophical poetry. He was the brother of the diarist Dorothy Wordsworth (1771–1855). His work includes: *The Lyrical Ballads*, 'The Ruined Cottage', 'Revolution and Independence', 'I wandered lonely as a cloud', 'Surprised by Joy', 'Lines Composed a Few Miles above Tintern Abbey', and 'The Prelude'.

'The Prelude' seems to set itself up as something of an egotistical project (it has an alternative title, 'Growth of a Poet's Mind', and a subtitle 'An Autobiographical Poem'). Unpublished during his lifetime, 'The Prelude' is an epic poem in fourteen books that tells the story of Wordsworth's life. The early books recount his childhood and school years. The middle books recall his time at Cambridge University and his subsequent life in London. Later sections detail his time in France and his mental crisis following the disappointment of his hopes for the revolution in 1789. The poem concludes with Wordsworth's retreat to the Lake District. The poem is important not only because it is said to represent some of Wordsworth's best poetry but because as a major autobiographical text it plays a significant role in constructing our understanding of the modern self. In this respect it resembles Rousseau's *Confessions* and is another key Romantic text for de Man. However, like Shelley's 'The Triumph of Life' it is also a philosophical poem, informed by the Enlightenment thinkers read by Wordsworth. The text is explicitly a philosophical investigation – in poetic form – into questions of consciousness and self-identity. Like any text it produces a form of knowledge but in so far as the story of Wordsworth's life is the story of European Romanticism, the knowledge the poem produces is of significant interest. *Essays on Epigraphs* might be read as a critical accompaniment to the philosophical positions adopted in 'The Prelude', but de Man turns this relation of subordination on its head. He suggests that not only are the essays chronologically contemporaneous with, but also logically prior to, the great poem and should be read as a prelude to 'The Prelude'. As with his account of Shelley, de Man's reading of these essays spends some time analysing the figure of the sun as a metaphor for knowledge.

De Man begins his essay by opening out our current understanding of the genre of autobiography. He states that the present study of autobiography is based on a set of problematic and restrictive assumptions. The first mistake is to imagine that autobiography is one literary genre among others. While the very idea of genre presupposes historical and aesthetic classifications (the novel, the epic, lyric poetry etc.) de Man suggests that what is at stake in autobiography is in fact 'the possible convergence of aesthetics and history [i.e. real events]' (*RR* 68). The second error is to think of autobiography as either historically fixed (if autobiography is impossible before the advent of modern consciousness, circa the eighteenth century, this excludes a fourth-century text like St Augustine's *Confessions*) or aesthetically fixed (current scholarship resists the idea of autobiographical poetry, thus excluding Wordsworth's 'The Prelude'). However, de Man focuses his attention on another difficulty, the supposed distinction between autobiography and fiction.

## AUTOBIOGRAPHY AND FICTION

Autobiography seems to depend upon the verifiability of the events it narrates, this is not the case for fiction. In this way it would seem to belong to a simpler, more transparently referential, mode of writing than fiction. Autobiography appears to be rooted in the certainty of the author whose identity confirms the meaning of the text. However, de Man wants to trouble this cosy understanding of autobiography, 'we assume that life *produces* the autobiography as an act produces consequences, but can we not suggest, with equal justice, that the autobiographical project may itself produce and determine the life' (*RR* 69). By this de Man does not mean that real events are determined by an author's desire to write a book. Rather, the 'life' narrated by autobiography is not necessarily the same life that was lead by the author, its narration is altered 'by the technical demands of self-portraiture and thus determined, in all its aspects, by the resources of [the] medium' (*RR* 69). However, de Man does not simply mean that authors rewrite events in order to appear better human beings in their autobiographies (this would be to re-instate the author as the conscious producer of meaning in a text). Rather, the writing of autobiography will be interrupted and disrupted by the arbitrary effects of language. Rousseau's *Confessions* are a good example of this (see pp. 41–6).

Citing the example of Proust's novel *A la recherche du temps perdu*, often assumed to be autobiographical, de Man suggests that it is never a straight-forward task to decide whether a moment in a novel is fictional or autobiographical. In fact, what we know about figuration suggests that it is impossible to decide whether figuration produces reference in a text or whether reference produces the figure. If this is the case, and all texts are figurative, then all texts are closer to an idea of fiction (i.e. that they are not simply referential) than we suppose. This leaves us in an undecideable situation, but asks de Man is it possible to remain in such a place? He notes, 'as anyone who has ever been caught in a revolving door or on a revolving wheel can testify, it is certainly most uncomfortable' (*RR* 70).

He proposes that autobiography 'is not a genre or a mode, but a figure of reading or of understanding that occurs, to some degree, in all texts' (*RR* 70). Autobiography happens when a text involves two persons constructing their own identities through reading each other. The author reads him/herself in autobiography, making themselves the subject of their own knowledge. This involves a form of substitution, exchanging the writing 'I' for the written 'I', and so implies that the two persons are at least as different as they are the same. De Man suggests that this 'specular structure' (two persons looking at each other) is interiorised within a text, i.e. it is no longer noticeable as such, like Nietzsche's coins. However, this structure is merely a special case of the situation that pertains in all texts. Whenever a text is said to be by someone (Wordsworth, Shelley, de Man etc.) it is thought to be understandable on this basis. For example, it is difficult to consider 'The Triumph of Life' without thinking of it as a text by Shelley and of having a specific biographical relation to Shelley. This, as de Man admits, 'amounts to saying that any book with a readable title page [e.g. 'The Triumph of Life by Percy Shelley'] is, to some extent, autobiographical' (RR 70).

However, de Man goes on to say in the next sentence that 'just as we seem to assert that all texts are autobiographical, we should say that, by the same token, none of them is or can be' (RR 70). The difficulty in defining autobiography as a closed genre (which would seem to exclude Augustine and Wordsworth) is merely a repetition of the difficulty of closure in any system of tropes. Autobiography defaces itself: any autobiographical text is inherently unstable and will undo the autobiographical model it seeks to establish. De Man returns to the metaphor of the revolving door to propose that its aptness suggests 'the turning motion of tropes' (RR 70). The specular structure of autobiography is 'the manifestation, on the level of referent [i.e. the life-story], of a linguistic structure' (RR 71). In so far as this structure of self-reading underlines all forms of knowledge, all understanding is produced by tropes. The interest of autobiography for de Man does not lie in the revelation of reliable self-knowledge (as in the case of Rousseau this seldom happens). Rather, autobiography 'demonstrates in a striking way the impossibility of closure and totalization ... [in] all textual systems made up of tropological substitutions' (RR 71).

## CLOSURE

An ending, the process of ending. Texts are said to achieve closure when they produce definite meanings that can be contained within the limits of the text. However, while we accept a conclusion as a working hypothesis in reading (we would not want to go on reading forever) any such attempt to curtail meaning is bound to fail. At the end of the film *Star Wars* the Death Star is destroyed and the Rebels hold a victory ceremony, thus providing an authoritative conclusion to the story. However, we know that the arch-villain Darth Vader has escaped to fight another day. This leads to the sequel *The Empire Strikes Back*. Within the single text of *Star Wars* the

> closing ceremony answers a need to end the film but leaves a number of
> outstanding threads (the price on Han Solo's head, the state of the rebel-
> lion as a whole) and so fails to provide closure.
>
> ## TOTALISATION
>
> An encapsulation, the process of encapsulation. A text or system is said
> to be totalising when it attempts to include all meaning within itself. For
> example, the Oxford English Dictionary attempts to define every word in
> the English language. However, if no text or system can achieve closure
> then it cannot produce an effective totalisation. An element will always
> remain outside of the text or system to challenge and undo its pretensions
> to totalisation. For example, the English language is always changing
> (under the influence of culture or other languages) and never remains
> fixed, thus the OED is in a continual state of revision and so fails in its
> own totalising project.

Autobiography relies on the identity and integrity of its author, the
reliability of its recollections, and the value of the self-knowledge it is
said to produce. However, autobiographical texts are keen to escape
'the coercions of this system' (*RR* 71). Autobiography is caught in the
double-bind between the necessity of escaping the authority of the
subject of autobiography (the written/writing-self which is merely a
tropological substitution) and the equal inevitability of reinscribing this
necessity into the 'specular structure' of knowledge which produces
autobiography. In this way, we might think of autobiography as an act
of self-restoration, in which the author recovers the fragments of
his/her life into a coherent narrative.

## AUTOBIOGRAPHY AND PROSOPOPEIA

During his close reading of the *Essays on Epitaphs* de Man identifies the
dominant trope of autobiography in Wordsworth as prosopopeia, 'the
fiction of an apostrophe [address] to an absent, deceased or voiceless
entity, which posits the possibility of the latter's reply and confers upon
it the power of speech' (*RR* 76). Prosopopeia is a 'voice-from-beyond-
the-grave' (*RR* 77) in which the dead are able to tell their own story, a

figure of speech which means 'face making'. In so far as autobiography recovers past – 'dead' – events and makes them speak in the form of a narrative, it is an exemplary rendition of prosopopeia. In this sense prosopopeia gives a mouth, and so a face, to a dead speaker. De Man seems to imply, although he does not explicitly state it, that all language works as a form of prosopopeia. Language is the means by which we construct our own masks of self-hood in the world. The gap between what is said and what it is described (characteristic of all language use, see pp. 34–8, 58) is like the fiction of a voice from beyond the grave conferring meaning on the past. Allegory (literally 'another speaking') is also a form of prosopopeia. De Man suggests that prosopopeia has an essential relation to defacement: to have a voice is to have a mouth is to have a face. The etymology of the word 'prosopopeia' comes from the Greek *prospon poien*, to confer a mask or a face (*prosopon*). Autobiography as prosopopeia 'deals with the giving and taking away of faces, with face and deface, *figure*, figuration and disfiguration' (*RR* 76). Autobiography disfigures the figure of prosopopeia and defaces the face it confers, disfiguring the mask it restores.

Characteristically de Man complicates this notion of autobiography as the making of a voice. In so far as the language of autobiography is figurative (prosopopeia) it is a representation of biography rather than the thing itself. As such, says de Man, 'it is silent, mute as pictures are mute' (*RR* 80). He suggests, 'language, as trope, is always privative' (*RR* 80), i.e. it always turns in on itself, disfiguring just as it figures. To the extent that we all depend upon figurative language we are all mute. All autobiography is mute, not 'silent' because this suggests the possible production of sound at our own will, but condemned to mute-ness by our implication within language. This paradox does not mean that no one can speak – obviously many of us can. Rather, if we under-stand that language is the means by which we posit face (self-hood) in the world then we will understand that the disruptive effects of figura-tive language do not deprive us of life but of the restoration of a coherent world with fixed and stable meanings. We cannot create a face that can never be disfigured.

This leads de Man to one of his most controversial conclusions:

> Death is a displaced name for a linguistic predicament, and the restoration of morality by autobiography (the prosopopeia of the voice and the name)

deprives and disfigures to the precise extent that it restores. Autobiography veils a defacement of the mind of which it is itself the cause.

(RR 81)

The first nine words here are often ripped from their context and used to demonstrate de Man's alleged extremism. However, as we can see, reading the full sentence and the complete essay the statement makes perfect sense. In so far as the death of a person involves their life being recast into a coherent narrative by those who mourn them (even if this narrative can be neither totalising nor achieve closure) this process is merely exemplary of language as a whole. Autobiography tells the story of a life – creating a face – but our day-to-day lives are also caught up in language, figurative language, which we use to shape and give meaning to those lives just as the figurative dimension of language unravels that meaning (defaces us). All autobiography must fail to be autobiographical (fail to produce a face incapable of disfigurement). Similarly, if autobiography is another 'allegory of reading' and indicative of language in general, all language will fail in its aim to bring sense and coherence to a life. The desire for coherence (which comes with the experience of mourning a dead person) and the simultaneous undoing of any such stability is the necessary condition of language. This is not an aberration but 'a linguistic predicament'.

## SUMMARY

In the two essays on Romantic poetry, 'Shelley Disfigured' and 'Autobiography as De-Facement', de Man pushes his understanding of rhetoric a stage further to complicate the arguments made in *Allegories of Reading*. The essays share a number of concerns:

- The transformation of literary texts into historical and aesthetic objects (the literary canon) involves a burying of those texts.
- Such texts become monuments to their dead authors. However, the figurative dimension of language at work in these texts disfigures these monuments.

- Disfiguration is a moment in a text when language both presents a figure or trope and begins to undo (disfigure) it.
- On the one hand, texts posit their own meaning and language has meaning because it articulates. On the other hand, language cannot possibly posit its own meaning since meaning is imposed on the arbitrary production of texts by readers who take them actually to refer to something.
- Autobiography is not a genre or a mode, but a figure of reading or of understanding that occurs, to some degree, in all texts.
- Any autobiographical text is inherently unstable and will undo the autobiographical model it seeks to establish.

# 5

# POLITICS, PHILOSOPHY AND THE FIGURAL

## *Aesthetic Ideology*

In the years before his death from cancer Paul de Man was attempting to further the arguments made in *Allegories of Reading* by a detailed examination of the texts of European philosophy (such as those of Blaise Pascal, Immanuel Kant, G.W.F Hegel, Friedrich Schiller, Walter Benjamin). This work is gathered together in the volume *Aesthetic Ideology*. This text was not published until 1996 although the essays have been available in periodical form since the 1980s. The essays in this book were given as a series of lectures at Cornell University and seem to have been intended as work in progress rather than a finished thesis. In an interview for Italian radio given in 1983 just after the lecture series (the text is reproduced in *The Resistance to Theory*) de Man outlined where his work was heading. In the lectures themselves de Man had made frequent reference to the book he was working on (it would have been his first major study since *Allegories*). It seems that this book would have taken the 'critical-linguistic analysis' or 'rhetorical reading' strategy of *Allegories* into an examination of the work of the German political theorist Karl Marx (1818–83) and the Scandinavian philosopher Søren Kierkegaard (1813–55). De Man explained that, even though he had been consistently misread by critics as an 'apolitical' theorist, his work is political through and through:

I don't think I ever was away from these problems, they were always uppermost in my mind. I have always maintained that one could approach the problems of ideology and by extension the problems of politics only on the basis of a critical-linguistic analysis, which had to be done in its own terms, in the medium of language, and I felt I could approach those problems only after having achieved a certain control over these questions.

(*RT* 121)

De Man's work does not seem to respond to the urgency of contemporary politics, but the paradox of philosophy is that to do justice to such urgency, philosophy must think through the 'urgency' and so ironically take its time over it. De Man's careful consideration of the problems of language in *Allegories* might be thought of as a prelude to thinking about the difficulty of ideology. The fact that de Man works out these issues over a lifetime of thinking does not make him any less committed to politics. On the contrary, thought cannot retard political action, it can only benefit it.

De Man's texts patiently and rigorously think through the complex relation between politics and language (the analysis of *The Social Contract* in *Allegories* would be a good example) just as his critics complacently deploy the rhetorical confusions which de Man identifies as the work of ideology. The book which de Man was preparing (provisionally entitled *Aesthetics, Rhetoric, Ideology*) focused on an analysis of Marx and Kierkegaard as the principal readers of Hegel's political philosophy. In preparation for this analysis de Man returned to the texts of Hegel himself and his predecessor Kant. This is the work that appears in the volume *Aesthetic Ideology*, which contains four of the intended nine chapters of *Aesthetics, Rhetoric, Ideology*. These essays have traditionally been under-read by scholars working in the field of so-called literary or critical theory, often dismissed as obscure and dense. While some sections of these essays are undoubtedly challenging, their difficulty is not a reason to ignore them. On the contrary, as de Man himself frequently demonstrates, such moments of textual difficulty call for close reading because their obscure meaning reveals the obscurity of meaning itself. However, for the reader of *Allegories* and *The Resistance to Theory* this work is certainly accessible. While de Man proposed to talk 'a little more openly' (*RT* 121) about politics in his later work, all of his texts are engaged with a similar theme, and it is not at all certain that the essays which de Man completed before his death make a significant ·advance on the work of *Allegories*. For this reason, this chapter will introduce some of the arguments made in *Aesthetic Ideology* by a return to certain themes in *Allegories of Reading* and *The Resistance to Theory*. This exposition of de Man's work will conclude with an examination of the general thesis of *Aesthetic Ideology*, namely, an account of the confusion between the figural and the literal which dominates the western political and philosophical traditions.

## AESTHETIC IDEOLOGY

The term 'Aesthetic Ideology' suggests a number of possible meanings, all of which are taken up by de Man:

1 Ideology, as a textual problem, is aesthetic.
2 Far from being neutral, natural or innocent, aesthetic objects (e.g. novels, paintings, music etc.) are ideological through and through.
3 'Aesthetics' as a philosophical and critical category is ideological.
4 Kant's and Hegel's famous texts on aesthetics have their own particular ideologies.
5 The traditional concepts of 'ideology', as used in Marxism, and 'aesthetics', as used in philosophy, rely on the same logocentric structure that is in need of deconstruction.
6 The problem of ideology (and by extension politics) can be approached by an understanding of aesthetics (and by extension textuality).
7 In other words, understanding ideology is a matter of reading.

## THE POLITICS OF PAUL DE MAN

De Man hints at the initial problem of ideology in the essay 'The Resistance to Theory'. There, following his remarks that language may not function according to the principles of the so-called 'real' world (see p. 53), he notes:

It would be unfortunate ... to confuse the materiality of the signifier [the unit of meaning such as words] with the materiality of what it signifies. ... What we call ideology is precisely the confusion of linguistic with natural reality, or reference with phenomenalism [objects themselves]. It follows that, more than any other mode of inquiry, including economics, the linguistics of literariness is a powerful and indispensable tool in the unmasking of ideological aberrations, as well as a determining factor in accounting for their occurrence. Those who reproach literary theory for being oblivious to social and historical (that is to say ideological) reality are merely stating their fear at having their own ideological mystifications exposed by the tool they are trying to discredit. They are, in short, very poor readers of Marx's *German Ideology*.

(*RT* 11)

De Man's rejoinder here may be read as a rebuke to those Marxist critics who, perhaps threatened by the implications of deconstruction for their own supposedly stable world-view, dismissed de Man's rhetorical analysis as detached from politics. De Man's work out-flanks such criticism, demonstrating that it is more Marxist than the Marxists. 'More Marxist' because it is based on an attentive reading of the text of Marx rather than a presumptive defence of alleged 'Marxist' truths.

## MARX AND IDEOLOGY

Karl Marx (1818–83): German political theorist, historian and economist who, along with Friedrich Engels (1820–95) provided an analysis of history as the struggle between competing classes. In 1848 Marx and Engels wrote *The Communist Manifesto*, an appeal to all workers to unite against the social structures that oppressed them. The political philosophy of Marxism is developed from the texts of Marx but Marx himself was the first person to say he was not a Marxist. His other works include: *Capital* (1867) *The German Ideology* (1845), *The Holy Family* (1884), *The Eighteenth Brumaire of Louis Napoleon* (1851).

Ideology, a key idea in Marx's texts, is the false representation of reality; it is the *idea* of a reality. In Marxism it is defined as 'false consciousness', as opposed to the true nature of reality, 'the system of ideas and representations which dominate the mind of a man or a social group' (Althusser 1977, 149). For example, in a capitalist society we are taught at school to work hard, be productive, and respect authority, thus training us to accept our future place in the work force. Ideology is not a set of rules or political dogmas (very often the term is lazily invoked in this way, for example when journalists speak of a politician's ideology).

Rather, as the structuralist Marxist Louis Althusser defines it, ideology 'represents the imaginary relationship of individuals to their real conditions of existence' (Althusser 1977, 153). The important terms here are 'represents' and 'imaginary', which suggest that ideology is in fact a linguistic and textual problem. Ideology is not a form of mind-control imposed upon the individual by external powers, rather it is the very way in which we live our lives: religious beliefs (theist or otherwise), political views, cultural identity, family history, supporting a football team, reading a newspaper, watching television and so on. All of which create an idea of reality, imagining the way we live out our roles as members of social classes by tying us to social functions through values, ideas, and images.

However, de Man is not necessarily interested in a simple division between ideology as a false view of the world and the supposed 'real' world. As we have seen throughout de Man's work he is keen to suggest that we do not have access to the 'real' world except through language. We would not recognise a table as a table unless we were already familiar with the concept of a table (what it is used for, how it is made, how it relates to other pieces of furniture and so on). We call a table a table because we understand and presuppose 'tableness' as a concept. However, as you will recall, the idea of a table is not necessarily natural to the thing it describes, rather it is a trope which metaphorically describes the thing we call a table. If language is figurative all the way down, no word is linked absolutely to the thing it describes. Rather, our understanding of what is real is actually the use of a complex system of tropes, which have meaning by reference to one another not the things they describe. In this way there remains an unbridgeable gap between our cognition of a table and the thing itself. The whole point of logocentricism, or the error of literalism, is to disguise or efface this gap. Thus what we take to be an experience of the material world (this is a table) is in fact an experience of the materiality of the word, or signifier, 'table' which gives the object meaning and makes it knowable.

In this way de Man extends the Marxist notion of ideology. Ideology is not a matter of shaking off a false consciousness and seeing the world as it truly is. Rather, what Marxism calls ideology is in fact the way all language works. For the purposes of living our lives we all inhabit the error of literalism and assume a straight-forward relation between a word like 'table' and the thing it describes. However, as we have seen repeatedly, to do so is to be caught up in a tropological system of language which undermines the trope of literalism just as much as it performs it. To confuse the linguistic reality of tropes and concepts with an actual experience of the real is, says de Man in 'The Resistance to Theory', precisely the action of ideology. Furthermore, the term 'ideology' is a trope used to figuratively describe this operation. Thus, we cannot say we are any closer to an experience of the real by using this term, rather we are once again suspended in language. There is no escape from this situation, language cannot pull itself up by its bootstraps. There is no escaping language by means of language.

The conclusion we can draw from this argument is that language itself is material, i.e. our use of language determines our experience of the real world. This is similar to Derrida's 'infamous' comment in *Of Grammatology* when he notes 'there is nothing outside the text' (*il n'y a pas de hors-texte*). This does not mean, as it has often been taken to mean, that reality does not exist or that readers should not be interested in supposedly 'extra-textual' concerns such as history, sociology, politics etc. Rather, it is a somewhat misleading translation of the French. A better translation of Derrida's phrase might be 'there is nothing text-free'. When we experience a table we are caught up in the problem of tropes and concepts, i.e. textuality. History and politics are themselves experienced through language, are themselves tropes, and so are textual from top to bottom. No absolute limit can be drawn between the text one reads, in Derrida's case it was Rousseau's *Confessions*, and the textuality of the history, sociology, and politics which inform it and are informed by it. Far from suggesting that one should ignore extra-textual matters Derrida says that, as a result of the over-spill of textuality, it is impossible for readers to avoid such matters. So, another way to translate this phrase might be 'there is nothing but context'. Not that the real world is a text, rather that as far as human beings, as users of language, are concerned the real world is always experienced textually. Thus, by de Man's account, his own critical-linguistic analysis (the word deconstruction is seldom used in these later essays in order to avoid becoming bogged down in the contentious reactions it provoked at the time) is well placed to provide a useful understanding of the political and ideological problems of material existence.

# THE MATERIALITY OF THE LETTER

In 'The Task of the Translator', the final lecture in the Messenger series given at Cornell, de Man uses the problems of translation to highlight what he calls 'the materiality of the letter' (*RT* 89). Translation is said to demonstrate the incompatibility of grammar and meaning. If the meaning of a sentence resided in its syntax alone then a literal translation of the sentence will produce the same meaning. We know this is not the case, such is the point of Benjamin's essay. De Man suggests that just as the meaning of a sentence does not lie in the individual words, the meaning of a word is not derived from its individual letters. 'When you spell a word you say a certain number of meaningless letters, which then come together in the word, but in each of the letters the word is not present' (*RT* 89). The meaning of the word 'fish' does not lie in any of its component letters – f, i, s, or h – but in its totality. For de Man the meaning of the letters and the meaning of the word are totally independent and incompatible. This disjunction between grammar and meaning 'is the materiality of the letter, the independence, or the way in which the letter can disrupt the ostensibly stable meaning of a sentence and introduce in it a slippage by means of which that meaning disappears, evances, and by means of which all control over that meaning is lost' (*RT* 89). In other words there is always a disjunction between the symbol and what it symbolises. Not only do we not experience the fish as such, we do not even connect with the letters of the word, rather we experience the illusion of totality of the trope 'fish'. This leads to another disjunction between the totalising ambition of a trope, which always wants to be taken for reality, and what a trope actually achieves as it performs its own deconstruction.

If language itself is material, our experience of the material is therefore open to all the aporias and impossibilities of deconstruction, which de Man's work identifies. An aporia is a rhetorical figure of doubt in which the conditions of possibility of an event or concept are, paradoxically, its own conditions of impossibility resulting in an interpretative impasse or moment of undecideability. For example, translation as the failure to translate (see pp. 61–2) involves a moment of aporia. To say that language is material is not simply a matter of returning to traditional notions of history and politics with the proviso that they are experienced as texts. Nor is it a matter of supposing that the world is one big text waiting to be read, because this assumes the readability that de Man is at such pains to interrogate. Rather, it means that the experience of the material will be as complex, undecideable, and irreducibly *unreadable* as the figurative language which produces it. This is a fundamental disruption of the conventional understanding of history and politics as it appears in the humanities, which always presupposed that both history and politics were knowable entities against which texts could be measured and verified. De Man's thinking of the materiality of the letter radically opens up these categories. Firstly, by demonstrating that they are textually inscribed and secondly, by showing that politics must always fail as politics (history as history). While we may assume that we know what we mean by a word like 'politics', the work of politics will demonstrate that we know no such thing.

For de Man the questions of politics cannot be asked outside of a consideration of aesthetics and philosophy. He notes in the essay 'Hegel on the Sublime', 'aesthetic theory is critical philosophy to the second degree, the critique of critiques. It critically examines the possibility and the modalities of political discourse and political action, the inescapable burden of any linkage between discourse and action' (*AI* 106). If the link between political discourse (reference) and political action (referent) is not guaranteed, and discourse and action cannot be mapped identically onto one another, then as a condition of under-standing the political field at all we must pay attention to this slippage between discourse (or language) and action. This means being critically aware of the ways in which discourse (texts, pronouncements, concepts) and action fail to meet up. Rather than being duped by the ideological manoeuvre that suggests making political or ethical pronouncements, or adhering to a political/ethical programme, while very necessary, is somehow sufficient to come to terms with the nature of the ethical or political. Furthermore, if any political action – which depends on the materiality of the letter for its understanding – can never be independent of an accompanying political discourse, then understanding the political will require a critical appreciation of textu-ality. If the aesthetic realm is the space in which the conditions of textuality are most readily visible then a questioning of politics must start here. But says de Man, following Hegel, 'the consideration of aesthetics only makes sense in the context of the larger question of the relationship between the order of the political and the order of philosophy' (*AI* 106).

De Man suggests that aesthetic study is 'a more advanced but proximate stage of speculative [philosophical] thought' (*AI* 107) than political reflection and so a productive political thought can be accessed through a critical appreciation of aesthetics. Aesthetics is both a more rigorous and a more provisional way of thinking than political discourse, which because of the demands made on it (the urgency to say something, the need to speak now) is always in a rush and must always enter into action as half-thought. Unlike political discourse aesthetics does not confuse its own identity with the action it describes and is therefore more aware of the gap between discourse and action, an awareness which is for de Man the very possibility of political thought. For example, we might read the elision of this gap within political discourse as a particularly powerful political manoeuvre itself, which screens out the textual nature of political programmes, an erasure that will always serve political interests. This ideological gesture disguises the rhetorical status of something like the texts of Marx or Adam Smith's *The Wealth of Nations* (it is a deception common to both left and right) and presents them as immediately connected to political action. A critical-linguistic analysis of politics would not only examine the gap between such texts and supposed political action, but the gap between any action and the tropological or linguistic means by which it is understood. That is to say, the fundamental disjunction between political events and our cognition of them. For example, we might examine the operation of a trope such as 'class', which has a conceptual history and is wholly figurative, while also coming to designate a distinct political phenomenon. Classes may exist but class is a concept open to deconstruction. Thus, for de Man, deconstruction 'is politically effective because of, and not in spite of, [its] concentration on literary [i.e. rhetorical] texts' (*AI* 107).

## THERE IS NOTHING TEXT-FREE

To say, as Derrida does, that there is nothing text-free does not mean that everything takes place in books, merely that there is no referent which is outside of the effects of textuality. The so-called 'real' world is a textual or rhetorical effect. De Man's deconstruction of politics examines the move common to all traditional political discourses, namely, that it is possible to step outside of rhetoric into the literal. Consider the Marxist critic Terry Eagleton's dismissal of de Man in his *Literary Theory: An Introduction* (1983), when he claims deconstruction views 'famines, revolutions, soccer matches and sherry trifle as yet more undecideable text' (146). Here Eagleton imagines that he is demonstrating the absurdity of deconstruction by juxtaposing the painfully real (famines and revolutions) with the frivolity of texts, while highlighting the danger of deconstruction's claims by collapsing his hierarchy of the real (famines, revolutions, soccer matches, sherry trifle) into the homogeneity of the text. In this formulation trifle is somehow, and somewhat tastelessly, less real or less important than famine, as if the existence of something as decadent as 'sherry trifle' in the west was not the cause of famine in Africa. The implication is that deconstruction's rhetorical interests are quite unable to explain the brute reality of a famine, while the act of recognising that famines are important things is a sufficient basis for radical politics. If only it were that easy.

In fact Eagleton here demonstrates the problem that de Man's work exposes. The list 'famines, revolutions, soccer matches and sherry trifle' may be an appeal to the literal but it is rhetorical from start to finish. The choice of 'famine' works as a metonym for 'political events which are important because people die', thus enabling Eagleton to claim the moral high-ground over de Man's self-indulgent textuality. 'Revolutions' are less important than 'famines', fewer people are killed, but metonymically it positions Eagleton's own writing in a tradition of Marxist activism, the earnestness of the activism mitigating the errors of the writing. 'Soccer matches' and 'sherry trifle' work metaphorically to suggest the ambivalence of deconstruction to the real or to power. Not that Eagleton has any particular interest in the relative merits of football and party food here. Rather these terms are invoked to demonstrate the serious and superior nature of his discourse because it is concerned with the literal. However, all that this sentence shows is the rhetorical nature of his argument and in fact the complete unimportance of the literal to his political position: famines and sherry trifle could easily be substituted for rhetorical equivalents such as floods and rice pudding.

Eagleton's text, and the traditional mode of political thought it represents, assumes that it is possible to step out of language into the literal. However, all Eagleton succeeds in showing is that such politics rely upon tropes, which successfully erase their own metaphorical status. Thus Eagleton's appeal to the literal wants to carry off language itself, to transport it into the real world (as if language did not always already exist in the real world). This transportation is itself a metaphor, a secondary operation of language – Eagleton denounces language by means of language. The literal is itself a metaphor and in traditional (logocentric) political discourse it becomes the metaphor of metaphors, the metaphor which is no longer seen as a metaphor. The literal does not stand alone as the criterion against which political discourse can be measured, as Eagleton assumes, but is one trope among many. This is not to deny 'literality' but to insist that, in the words of the British critic and theorist Bill Readings, 'the literal cannot ground itself outside of rhetoric' (Waters and Godzich 1989, 229). We cannot know the real outside of language, thus the real must always be understood in terms of the figural. The real is always rhetorical. The distinction between the literal and the figural is an effect of language not a given fact of the natural world.

## AESTHETIC IDEOLOGY

Most of the essays in *Aesthetic Ideology* follow an argument through the philosophy of Kant and Hegel, who recognise that an understanding of aesthetics is a necessary condition of a philosophical inquiry into politics.

It can be argued that aesthetics, or representation, is the crucial link between real events and philosophical texts (if you like, between materialism and idealism). De Man argues that far from formulating an

### IMMANUEL KANT (1724–1804)

German Enlightenment philosopher whose work attempts to reconcile idealism and materialism, i.e. a philosophy which explores the tension between the impossibility of knowing a 'thing-in-itself' outside of our own understanding (idealism) and the necessity that the 'thing-in-itself' correspond to our representation of it (materialism). Kant proposes that knowledge is not the aggregate of encounters with the material world but is dependent on the conceptual apparatus of our own understanding, which is not itself derived from experience. Author of *Critique of Pure Reason* (1781), *Critique of Practical Reason* (1788) and *Critique of Judgement* (1790). His work was the subject of a polemical attack by Hegel.

## GEORG WILHELM FRIEDRICH HEGEL (1770–1831)

German philosopher who established dialectics as a mode of modern philosophical inquiry. Dialectics supposes all phenomena to be in the process of perpetual change, contradiction, and development. As a method dialectics seeks to reconcile two contradictions into a third greater knowledge. Hegel uses dialectics to investigate the conditions of thought (idealism), later Marx and Engels will develop a materialist form of dialectics. Author of *Phenomenology of Spirit* (1807), *Encyclopaedia of the Philosophical Sciences* (1817), *Lectures on Aesthetics* (1820), and *Philosophy of Right* (1826). Both Kant and Hegel are key thinkers in the development of *aesthetics*, the branch of philosophy (emerging in the eighteenth century) which deals with the nature of beauty, especially in art.

adequate notion of aesthetics that will help them develop their philosophical systems, Kant and Hegel's texts succeed in undoing the aesthetic as a valid philosophical category. Thus Kant and Hegel cannot close off their philosophical systems because they cannot ground their discourse on a principle internal to the system. Because the system cannot be closed it cannot be systematic or insure its absolute correctness or authority. In attempting to validate the aesthetic, the texts of Kant and Hegel present the aesthetic as a trope which deconstructs, or disarticulates, itself. De Man's strategy for reading here will be familiar to those who have followed his analysis of the promise or the confession in *Allegories of Reading* (see pp. 41–6). However, de Man takes his formulation of the 'metaphorical-metonymical tropological system' a step further in these essays (at least explicitly, for this was always implied in *Allegories*). De Man proposes that the disarticulation of the category of the aesthetic takes place in a material way.

For example, de Man suggests that while Hegel's *Aesthetics* is 'dedicated to the preservation and the monumentalisation of classical art, it also contains all the elements which make such a preservation impossible from the start' (*AI* 102). In de Man's reading of Hegel, the paradigm for art in the Aesthetics 'is thought rather than perception, the sign rather than the symbol, writing rather than painting or music' (*AI* 103) – in other words, things that may seem external to the aesthetic experience. Hegel's definition of the beautiful is the occurrence to the mind of 'the sensory appearance of the Idea' and yet throughout his text he suggests that this experience occurs in moments (writing, thinking, learning by rote rather than internalised memory) which all imply some sense of inscription. That is to say, they do not rely on an immediate and transparent experience of the aesthetic as a natural category, but on a general system of meaning, which presupposes the aesthetic as a concept or trope before the work of art is created or experienced (see the discussion of inscription on pp. 21–3).

Thus Hegel's text combines two seemingly contradictory theses: 'art is the sensory appearance of the Idea', 'art is for us a thing of the past'. De Man argues that these two statements turn out to be the same thing. Art is of the past because it is radically separate from the interiorisation of experience (i.e. the immediate and transparent experience of art as naturally beautiful). Art is of the past because it materially inscribes and thus, in the sense of forgetting invoked by de Man's essay on Shelley (see pp. 68–9), forgets its ideal content. By material inscription we mean the experience of the 'real' as a textual effect of the general system of meaning, thus our experience of the material and our imbrication within textuality is one and the same. This forgetting makes the ideal content that which the art object would like us to be aware of but which it can never retrieve. For example, a painting such as Giotto's fresco 'Charity', discussed in de Man's reading of Proust in *Allegories of Reading* (see p. 35), asks us to think about charity but is unable to impress this ideal content upon us because the moment the painting enters into meaning (language, inscription) it opens up to ambiguity and misreading. The reconciliation of these two statements must come at the expense of the aesthetic as a stable category. The point at which this disarticulation, or deconstruction, of the category of the aesthetic occurs is at the moment of inscription which for de Man is a material occurrence. As he states in the essay 'Phenomenality and Materiality in Kant', 'the prosaic materiality of the letter' is something which 'no degree of obfuscation or ideology can transform ... into the phenomenal cognition of aesthetic judgement' (*AI* 90). That is to say, material inscription (what Derrida calls 'Writing', see pp. 21–3) deconstructs the ideological ruse of the aesthetic as a natural phenomenon.

However, de Man argues throughout these essays that the deconstruction of the category of the aesthetic comes about not as a weakness in Kant's and Hegel's argument but as a consequence of the rigour of their argument. The idea that the aesthetic is something natural or immediate, de Man argues, comes about as a result of the German philosopher Friedrich Schiller's (1759–1805) misreading of Kant and Hegel. This misreading enters into the philosophical tradition after Schiller as the standard interpretation of Kant and Hegel. The texts of Kant and Hegel however, according to de Man, are not caught up in this aesthetic ideology (which is essentially a logocentric under-standing of the aesthetic as an immediately experienced phenomenon, which erases the status of the aesthetic as a trope). De Man argues that for Kant and Hegel the aesthetic is only ever a trope because it must play a rhetorical role in their conceptual system, to unite the political and the philosophical. The fact that this deconstruction of the aesthetic actually takes place in these texts means for de Man that it constitutes a 'real event', something that happens. Thus the texts of Kant and Hegel have a material history, or are history – an event – and so have a future. What does not happen in the texts of Kant and Hegel, and so cannot be historical or be said to have a future, is the ideological manoeuvre of turning the aesthetic into an immediate experience, which de Man identifies with Schiller.

## THE MATERIAL EVENT OF READING

Schiller's misreading of Kant and Hegel is significant because it remains today the dominant mode of thinking about the aesthetic. It has a double influence. Firstly, we might consider what ideological or tropo-logical operation is at work whenever we say or are told, this is great literature/art/music/architecture etc. The justification of such canoni-sation, and the assumption that a canon of literature or art exists (even though it may have been expanded recently to include women or non-white authors) remains the fundamental task of critical study in the humanities. It is a project that relies unquestioningly on the category of the aesthetic, while being unable to account for or recognise the aesthetic. In this sense if the 'human sciences' are unable to read them-selves, they can no longer be called a science but approach the status of something like an allegory of science. Secondly, it is the unrecognised ideology of the aesthetic as 'the beautiful' rather than the mundane and ordinary, which underpins the assumption that the figurative or rhetor-ical is a category distinct from the literal and peculiar to art. As we have seen above, this has pronounced consequences for thinking about the political and the literal. In short, aesthetic ideology is the name de Man gives to the belief that the figural and the literal are separate realms.

De Man is not proposing Kant or Hegel (or himself for that matter) as demystifing critiques of ideology – somehow smarter than the poor fools duped by ideology. As Althusser suggests, we are never so much in ideology as when we believe ourselves to be outside it. These texts are said to be material precisely because they do not transcend the ideological circumstances under which they are read. They do not provide us with some external vantage point from which to look down upon ideology or to exert critical leverage on other ideology-bound texts. This would be merely to repeat the gesture of someone like Eagleton above who follows a traditional philosophical model of 'ideology-critique' by believing himself to be outside of the ideology he criticises. Rather, the disarticulation of the aesthetic happens in these texts in such a way as to make impossible the closure of the philosophical system, which puts the category of the aesthetic into play. There can be no closure to the system and so no escape from it. Thus there is no vantage point from which to view the system other than one from within the system itself, i.e. one which is itself always in disarticulation (both forming and deconstructing the category of the aesthetic). As de Man states in 'Phenomenality and Materiality in Kant', 'the critical power of transcendental philosophy [Kant and Hegel's attempt to formulate the aesthetic as a concept which would regulate their entire philosophical system] undoes the very project of such a philosophy' (*AI* 89).

Kant and Hegel do not provide us with an account of aesthetic ideology but rather these texts are precisely the historical conditions under which such an ideology is produced (by Schiller's misreading) and, at the same time, disarticulated. The inability of transcendental philosophy to achieve transcendence leaves the texts of Kant and Hegel as not so much a 'philosophical system' as an allegory of philosophy. What these texts show is that while tropes remain the material conditions for the possibility of such a conceptual system, a rhetorical reading of a text is never sufficient in itself to account for a text. A rhetorical reading is a real event which is always caught up in the event it reads. This means that a text cannot be reduced solely to tropes, there remains irreducible to each text the material event of its disarticulation. While, the metaphorical-metonymical tropological system of language is responsible for this disarticulation, a rhetorical reading of such an event cannot escape the linguistic system which produces it. A rhetorical reading cannot be a form of ideology-critique. A rhetorical reading cannot be a totalitarian reading even though the ambition of tropes tends towards totalisation. Just as there can be no closure to the material event of disarticulation there can be no total reading of this event. What de Man's understanding of aesthetic ideology alerts us to is the complicity between the literal as a trope (the dream of totality) and totalitarian systems of thought. De Man's last essays point to a way of deconstructing totalitarianism, but it could well be argued that this was also the lesson of *Blindness and Insight*.

## SUMMARY

De Man's final essays on European philosophy, collected in *Aesthetic Ideology*, point towards the political consequences of his thought:

- Ideology is the confusion of linguistic with natural reality, or reference with the objects referred to.
- What we take to be an experience of the material world is in fact an experience of the materiality of language, which gives the world meaning and makes it knowable.
- If language itself is material, our experience of the material is therefore open to all the undecideabilities and impossibilities of deconstruction, which de Man's work identifies.
- There is no meaning that is outside of the effects of textuality.
- The real is always rhetorical. The distinction between the literal and the figural is an effect of language not a given fact of the natural world.
- Aesthetic ideology is the belief that the figural and the literal are separate realms.
- Deconstruction cannot be a totalising way of reading. It is always caught up in the event that it reads, unable to escape the ideological conditions of that reading.
- Deconstruction is a disarticulation of all totalitarianism(s).

# 6

# RESPONSIBILITY AND AUTHORSHIP

## De Man's wartime journalism

In August 1987, four years after the death of Paul de Man, the German philosopher and literary critic Samuel Weber telephoned Jacques Derrida to speak to him about a disturbing discovery. Weber had just returned from a conference in Belgium where he had met a Belgian student called Ortwin de Graef. While preparing for his doctoral dissertation on de Man, de Graef had come across articles written by the critic in two newspapers, the French language *Le Soir* and the Flemish language *Het Vlaamsche Land*, during the German occupation of Belgium between 1941 and 1942 when de Man was 22 years old. These newspapers had been sympathetic to the German occupation. De Graef was well aware of what would happen, especially in America, on the publication of his findings. Weber told Derrida that de Graef had sought his advice on how best to handle the situation and hoped that Weber would also seek Derrida's opinion. However, by the time Weber spoke to Derrida, de Graef had already communicated his discovery to other scholars in America – notably at Yale – and had sent translations of four texts to the British journal *Textual Practice*. Weber and Derrida decided to ask de Graef – who was about to start his military service in Belgium – to send them copies of all the articles in French that he had found, after which they would offer an opinion. De Graef sent them a selection of 25 texts with a bibliography of 125 further texts, which he could not send for technical reasons. Derrida and Weber wanted to complete the work that de Graef could not finish and decided to publish all the accessible articles, making them available to as wide an audience as possible.

The articles caused a media sensation. For some it was unthinkable that a leading member of the Yale School of deconstruction had been associated with the collaborationist press in occupied Europe; for others it proved what they had always suspected about the political credentials of deconstruction. It is clear that many who rushed into print to denounce de Man as a Nazi had not read the articles and had made up their minds about them before they were ever published. The logic ran: de Man wrote for *Le Soir* during the war therefore he must be a Nazi, therefore the whole of deconstruction is Nazism. De Man's detractors also repeated a series of errors about deconstruction and reported factual inaccuracies about his life. The attacks came from an odd mix of traditional literary critics and philosophers, Marxist critics (who had an axe to grind with deconstruction) and outraged journalists. There was a tone of gleeful vengeance in much of the journalism that commented on what became known as the 'de Man affair', as those opposed to deconstruction took this opportunity to make a public denunciation of de Man and everything he represented.

The trial of Paul de Man was conducted, in his absence, in the media, which has little time for the patient study of difficult texts of literary criticism. The sensational story was everything, the texts themselves of little importance. Two examples give some idea of the attacks on de Man. The Marxist critic Jeffrey Mehlman wrote:

> For de Man, it now appears, served, in the course of his life, as champion of two radical cultural movements from abroad: as partisan of the Nazi 'revolution' among the Walloons in the 1940s [N.B. de Man was actually Flemish] and as an advocate of 'deconstruction' among the Americans in the 1970s. ... De Man's fling with anti-Semitism ... was not a good-faith error, but an indulgence in deception. His subsequent reputation for probity – exercised over the years in discrimination between the first and second rate in American academia – no doubt deserves to suffer as a consequence.

(Hamacher *et al.* 1989, 324, 326)

Geoffrey Hartman, a Yale colleague of de Man, wrote a defence of de Man's later work and character, to which the journalist Jacob Neusner replied in *The Jewish Advocate* on 31 March 1988:

> Hartman uses every trick of the trade to shift attention from a fact he wishes would go away: that his teacher, colleague, and friend hated Jews and was a Nazi. ... To deconstructionism, things are what you say they are. So up is down and black is white and east is west and somehow this disreputable and disgusting Nazi, de Man, has been turned into a man of conscience, no less. ... No Jew can admire Hartman for writing this way about a vicious anti-Semite and Nazi collaborator.

As is clear from these quotations, the critics were also reacting to the positions taken by de Man's friends on the newly discovered texts. After careful consideration of all of de Man's wartime writing a number of prominent names within deconstruction contributed to the volume, *Responses to Paul de Man's Wartime Journalism 1940–1942*, edited by Werner Hamacher, Neil Hertz and Thomas Kennan, published in 1989. This collection accompanied the publication of all of de Man's wartime texts in a separate volume in 1988. The essays in the responses book are by turn poignant and painful, expressing genuine hurt and shock at the revelation of de Man's (who was a friend of most of the contributors) part in the collaborationist press. The arguments of each of the essays tend to cover the same ground, calling for close reading of all of de Man's texts and stressing the ways in which the mature work of de Man differs from his youthful error. There is a general willingness to forgive de Man, even if none of the essays attempts to ignore the distressing nature of what he wrote. Meanwhile, a number of people who had known de Man during the war came forward to vouch for the probity of his activities during this time. Among them were members of the resistance.

Jacques Derrida, in 'Like the Sound of the Sea Deep Within a Shell: Paul de Man's War' (1988) suggested four 'rules' for reading de Man's wartime journalism, which can be summarised as follows:

1   Reconstitute as much of the text 'Belgium during the war' as possible. This should include internal as well as contextual issues; avoid giving the articles in question a disproportionate importance by minimising the rest.
2   Relate the wartime writing to de Man's later deconstruction while avoiding two symmetrical errors: that of saying that there is absolutely no relation between them whatsoever, and that of asserting complete identity between them, treating them as

exactly the same thing as if Paul de Man did not have a history and were not allowed to change his mind.

3   Respect the other's right to difference, to error, to aberration and mistake. Above all respect de Man's right to a history. One sign of such respect would be to begin to listen.

4   Avoid as much as possible reproducing the logic of the discourses being attacked: Nazi, fascist, anti-Semitic, totalitarian, collaborationist. This will only be possible if one is able to identify not only the similarities between these discourses but also the differences.

This chapter will explore the contexts of de Man's wartime journalism. This information, alongside the previous chapters of the book, will equip readers to follow through Derrida's other suggestions and, eventually, to make independent judgements on 'the de Man affair'.

## PAUL DE MAN, HENRI DE MAN AND WARTIME BELGIUM

De Man's Belgian biography has proved as fascinating as his American critical texts. His uncle, Henri de Man, was a prominent Belgian politician and socialist theorist who played a significant role in the choices Paul de Man made during the wartime occupation of Belgium by the Nazis. In 1933, when de Man was 14, Hitler became Chancellor of Germany. In the same year Henri de Man left the University of Frankfurt where he was a professor of social psychology and became involved in socialist and anti-fascist activities. He returned from Germany to teach at the Université Libre de Bruxelles and became vice-president of the Belgian socialist party, which entered into a coalition government in 1935. In 1936 three significant events occurred within a month of each other: the death of Paul de Man's brother, Hendrick, in a cycling accident, the appointment of Henri de Man as Minister of Finance (the second most important post in the Belgian government), and the outbreak of the Spanish Civil War. The clouds of war were gathering over Europe and the de Man family found themselves torn between public duty and private tragedy. The following summer, de Man's mother committed suicide.

In October 1937 Paul de Man entered the École Polytechnique in

Brussels to study engineering. He joined the Cercle du Libre Examen, a left-wing student group at the Université Libre de Bruxelles with the declared position 'libre-exameniste [free thinking], democratic, anti-clerical, antidogmatic, and antifascist'. Following the German annexation of Austria in 1938 (the *Anschluss*) Henri de Man resigned his post as Minister of Finance. Throughout his degree Paul de Man had maintained close links with his uncle and his cousin. When the time came for de Man to take his exams to graduate he did not do so, instead he transferred to the Faculty of Science at Université Libre de Bruxelles (the liberal Protestant university) to study chemistry and became increasingly involved with the Cercle du Libre Examen. On the 29th of September the Munich Pact was signed ceding the German-speaking provinces of Czechoslovakia (the Sudetenland) to the Third Reich, temporarily averting war. In December of that year Henri de Man undertook a peace mission on behalf of the Belgian King, Leopold III, and other neutral countries in an attempt to resolve German territorial demands. It was abandoned in March 1939 when German troops occupied the whole of Czechoslovakia, making war all but inevitable.

At this time Paul de Man was a young man caught up in political events few could understand and no one seemed able to control. He was caught between his studies, student politics, the increasing draw of literature, and falling in love with his future wife Anaïde Baraghian (they married in May 1944). He began to write for the journal of the Cercle Libre du Examen, *Jeudi*, and joined the editorial board of the *Cahiers du Libre Examen*, the group's other publication. War broke out in September 1939, by which time Henri de Man had become the President of the Belgian socialist party. After Hitler's invasion of Poland, Henri de Man joined a new government of national unity, which held to a policy of strict neutrality. On the outbreak of war the Cercle du Libre Examen voted to expel its Stalinist members, following the Nazi–Soviet non-aggression pact which had allowed Germany and the Soviet Union to divide Poland between them. These same Soviet-affiliated students would later brand Paul de Man a Nazi sympathiser.

In 1940 de Man's uncle left the government to serve in the military as a captain attached directly to the King's service. Perhaps under his uncle's influence, Paul de Man wrote several articles in *Jeudi* and *Cahiers* in support of Belgian neutrality and against a military alliance with France and Britain. The argument for Belgian neutrality was not based on pacifist principles but on pragmatic grounds. The reasoning ran that a country of Belgium's size could not possibly defeat the German war machine and in any conflict would be swamped, regardless of alliances. The best way to preserve Belgian territory, culture, and lives was to remain neutral. De Man became editor of *Cahiers du Libre Examen* and edited its two final issues on 'Western Civilisation' and 'Totalitarianism'. On 10 May, after rejecting offers of military intervention by Britain and France, Belgium was invaded by Germany. While some ministers in the government fled to Paris to set up a government in exile, an exodus of two million Belgians fled south through France. Paul de Man and Anaïde Baraghian were among them, spending the summer in the Pyrenees, waiting unsuccessfully for permission to cross into neutral (but fascist) Spain. On the advice of Henri de Man, and in order to avoid bloodshed, King Leopold III surrendered the Belgian army to the Germans. A German military administration was set up to rule Belgium, unlike Holland and later France which were run by collaborationist civilian regimes.

One of the Germans' first actions in Belgium was to take control of all newspaper, periodical, and book production. This included the biggest Belgian daily newspaper *Le Soir*. The German authorities installed a new editorial staff, and the paper was derisively known among Belgians as *Le Soir volé* (the stolen evening). All publications were subject to strict censorship before printing. All anti-German literature and particularly of the work of Jewish writers was systematically targeted. *Jeudi* and *Cahiers du Libre Examen* did not resume publication after the invasion. On 19 June 1940 France surrendered to Germany and later signed an armistice which placed half the country under German military occupation and half the country under the collaborationist Vichy civil administration. With the British retreat at Dunkirk and the Soviet Union's own invasion of Finland complete, the war – for occupied Belgians – seemed all but over and German victory a reality.

In July 1940 Henri de Man, as President of the Belgian socialist party, issued a manifesto to its members, saying 'do not believe it is necessary to resist the occupant; accept the fact of his victory and try to draw lessons from it ... for the working classes and for socialism, this collapse of a decrepit world, far from a disaster is a deliverance ... consider the political role of the Parti Ouvrier Belge [Belgian socialist party] as finished.' He may have been naïve enough to equate his own socialism with National Socialism, or, he may have wished to avoid further bloodshed, but this proclamation came at a time when the future of Belgium was uncertain and Henri de Man thought there was some possibility of salvaging Belgian culture and its institutions from the occupier. He thought that Belgium may even be allowed to exist as an autonomous state within the Third Reich. Hitler's orders for the occupation read, 'The Führer has not reached a definite decision concerning the future of the Belgian state. For the time being, he wishes all possible consideration for the Flemish, including the return of the Flemish prisoners of war to their homeland. No favour should be accorded to the Walloons [the French-speaking inhabitants of Southern Belgium].' After the defeat of France the Flemish Paul de Man and the Romanian Anaïde Baraghian returned to Brussels.

In October 1940 de Man changed degrees again, transferring to the programme in social sciences to read philosophy. In the same month the German military command in Belgium issued its first major decrees against Jews, requiring them to register with the authorities and banning them from public life. In November the Gestapo interrogated de Man at his flat about his involvement with Cercle du Libre Examen, but no action was taken.

## DE MAN'S JOURNALISM

On Christmas Eve 1940 Paul de Man's first article appeared in *Le Soir*. He was still a student at Université Libre de Bruxelles, but was now 21 and living with his partner, with a child on the way. If he worked elsewhere there was the possibility of being volunteered for the German economy, while at *Le Soir* he was offered a position of responsibility and critical freedom unheard of under normal circumstances for someone of de Man's youth. The suspicion remains that he probably obtained his position as a contributor through the influence of his uncle. De Man published 170 articles during his time at *Le Soir*, submitting pieces on literature, music, and culture on a freelance basis. German censorship had by now slipped to a policy of censoring subversive texts after they appeared. Only important political articles were still censored in advance.

De Man seems to have settled into an easy family life at this time, showing affiliations with neither the resistance nor collaborationist groups. His wartime journalism is generally uninteresting in itself. It consists of reviews of literature and art of the 1940s using the analytic tools of humanist criticism and literary history common at the time. There is a penchant for German literature and perhaps an over-stated dislike of French literature (this would change for the mature de Man). There are discussions of the future of Belgian culture after the occupation and occasional praise for the strength of German culture. Most of it is inoffensive and ambivalent about the collaborationist views held by the editors of *Le Soir*. If these texts had not been written by a young Paul de Man they would be of no interest outside of a study of Flemish culture of the 1940s. However, in several notable passages the tone is more engaged with the collaborationist agenda than one would hope for from Paul de Man. For example, on 25 March 1941 de Man wrote of the occupation:

> Eyes were opened on a hard reality: the reassuring speeches of governments which were customarily taken at their word turned out to be the worst sort of brainwashing, the force of the democracies believed to be intact appeared in the true light of day, the conventional image of the barbarous and malevolent enemy, created by systematic propaganda, collapsed before the impeccable conduct of the highly civilised invader.
>
> (Quoted Hamacher *et al.* 1989, 410)

Such comments have to be read in the context of the entire article in which it appears (an attempt to account for the dizzying events of 1940) which must also be read in the context of the entire wartime writing. However, the passage is an indication of the shock that the revelation of this journalism caused among de Man's associates and the type of ammunition it provided for his detractors.

Out of all of the articles one text stands out, it is entitled 'Les Juifs dans la Littérature actuelle' ('The Jews in Contemporary Literature', included as an appendix to this book). It is remarkable for several reasons. Firstly, because its seeming anti-Semitic tone seems so far removed from everything that is known about the Yale School de Man, friend of the Jewish thinkers Jacques Derrida, Geoffrey Hartman, and Harold Bloom. Secondly, because it is the only significant moment in the whole of de Man's wartime journalism which flirts with anti-Semitism. Thirdly, because its disturbing anti-Semitic argument is so blatantly self-contradictory (Derrida has used these inconsistencies to suggest that the text might be aware of its own difficulties and in some way resisting the anti-Semitic ideology it proposes) that it turned what was a drab collection of juvenilia by a Yale professor into a media incident. The article appeared in *Le Soir*, signed by de Man, in March 1941 as part of a 'special edition' to promote anti-Semitism. It seemed to suggest that the canon of western literature would not be greatly impoverished if all its Jewish authors were removed, concluding that '[the literary life of the West] would lose, in all, a few personalities of mediocre value and would continue, as in the past, to develop according to its great evolutive laws'. The argument of the article is tortuous and self-contradictory. At one point de Man cites Kafka as an example of good 'non-Jewish' writing. He must have known that Kafka was Jewish. Reports suggest de Man's reluctance to contribute to this edition but ultimately he chose to do so for fear of losing his job, with the threat of forced labour in Germany still a possibility.

By now de Man's contemporaries at Cercle du Libre Examen had gone their separate ways. Some collaborated with the Germans (to greater and lesser degrees), some joined the resistance, and some were either jailed or shot. The first armed resistance to the occupiers did not take place until June 1941.

A defeated and contrite Henri de Man published his political memoirs, *Après Coup*, in May 1941. It was the first book published by Toisin d'Or, a publishing house run by the editor-in-chief at *Le Soir* and backed by the German Foreign Office. By July Henri de Man was banned from speaking in public by the German authorities, and in November he left Belgium to live in occupied France. He returned to Belgium periodically but remained in touch with the resistance. In September 1941 Paul de Man along with three other former members of Cercle du Libre Examen were denounced as collaborators, for working at *Le Soir*, in an underground student journal, *L'Étudiant*. Having failed to take his final exams, de Man's education was interrupted when the Université Libre de Bruxelles was closed down after refusing to accept German intervention. He was left with only his qualification in chemistry.

By the start of 1942 the Nazi persecution of the Jews was gathering momentum and in January the Nazis made plans for the extermination of European Jews, including the 43,000 Jews resident in Belgium. In February, de Man, no longer a student and having to work full time, took up a post at the Agence Dechenne, a publishing house specialising in art and literature. De Man contributed book reviews to its journal *Bibliographie Dechenne*. While at the press de Man used his position to find work for Jewish friends (writing under pseudonyms) and friends associated with the resistance who could not find work elsewhere. De Man also held the post of reader at Toison d'Or with responsibility for selecting works for publication and hiring translators. Again he used this position to find work for friends blacklisted by the regime. In March de Man began to write the first of his ten articles for *Het Vlaamsche Land*, another Flemish daily newspaper printed on presses controlled by the Germans.

In June 1942 the second volume of Henri de Man's memoirs, *Réflexions sur la paix (Reflections on Peace)*, was seized and banned by the military authorities despite pre-publication approval with Toison d'Or. The head of the SS Heinrich Himmler set a quota of 10,000 Belgian Jews for deportation to concentration camps in Germany and Eastern Europe and by late July this process had begun in earnest. Paper shortages meant that *Le Soir* was reduced to only four pages in each edition, by the autumn this would be cut further with three of the six weekly editions appearing on only two sides of paper. At the same time the Propaganda Abteilung Belgien tightened restrictions on newspapers, reimposing the requirement that all articles be censored prior to publication and introducing a new prohibition against discussing the future form of the Belgian state. This had been a principal topic in the writing of the young Paul de Man and his more famous uncle.

At a time when the Germans had begun searching houses for Jews in hiding, Paul de Man and his partner sheltered for several days two Jewish friends who had been accidentally locked out of their apartment after the curfew hours imposed by the Germans. De Man repeated this gesture on other occasions during the occupation. By the autumn of 1942 the seemingly irreversible victory of the Germans began to look less secure. Germany had invaded the Soviet Union the previous year and America entered the war in December 1941. Losses on the eastern front and the increased pressure on the German war machine caused by fighting the Soviets while continuing to occupy western Europe, began to suggest that a reversal of fortunes may still be possible. In a radio broadcast from London the Belgian government in exile offered an amnesty to all journalists working for collaborationist newspapers who stopped writing by the end of the year. Whether as a consequence of this announcement or out of disillusionment with the increased levels of censorship, De Man's last article for *Het Vlaamsche Land* appeared in October and his last published article in *Le Soir* appeared in November. While visiting Brussels in November Henri de Man learned that his name was on a list of potential German hostages. He returned illegally to France where he was arrested by the Gestapo but released after the intervention of friends on the clear understanding that he cease all political activities. He spent the rest of the war in the French Alps.

With the Allied victory at El Alamein in North Africa (October 1942) and the surrender of the German army at Stalingrad in February 1943 the course of the war had turned. In March 1943 de Man was sacked from Agence Dechenne for helping to employ unsuitable persons and for arranging the publication of an edition of *Messages: Cahiers de la poésie française*, a subversive poetry magazine which had been refused publication by the German censors in Paris. In May an edition of *Poésie '43*, a French review which published poets of the resistance, reported that 'a palace revolution has removed from the directorship of certain publishing houses Georges Lambrichs and Paul de Man, who had defended new currents in French literature'. As the war turned, Belgian resistance became more daring, with attacks on a number of collaborationist journalists. Louis Frosny a former member of Cercle du Libre Examen and politico-literary contributor to *Le Soir* was shot dead by the resistance in January 1943. His assassination was celebrated in the resistance newspaper *L'Insoumis*, which also published a denunciation of forty-four journalists of *Le Soir (volé)*, including Paul de Man even though he had not written for *Le Soir* for eleven months prior to publication. De Man and his young family left Brussels in December 1943 and spent the rest of the war living with de Man's father in Antwerp. De Man spent much of his time preparing a translation of Herman Melville's novel *Moby Dick*.

In July 1944 the last Brussels to Auschwitz convoy left Belgium. Out of an approximated 66,000 Jews in Belgium 35,000 of them had been deported and 29,000 of them murdered by the end of the war. The German army was in full retreat by August and Brussels was liberated by Allied forces on 3 September 1944. In the days immediately following the liberation de Man was denounced in *Debout*, the journal of the Fédération des Etudiant Socialiste Unifés, along with other left-wing students at the pre-war Université Libre de Bruxelles who had worked in the occupation press and publishing. In May 1945, after the final defeat of Germany, de Man was called before the military prosecutor at the Palais de Justice in Antwerp for a day of questioning about his activities during the occupation. He was released without charge. A report of the Auditeur Général read, 'Paul de Man was not the object of charges brought before the Conseil de Guerre for his attitude or his activity during the war.' Other journalists at *Le Soir* were executed or imprisoned for their wartime writings.

After the war Paul de Man set up his own publishing house, Éditions Hermès, specialising in art books. Henri de Man was sentenced in his absence to twenty years imprisonment for his role in the defeat of Belgium. When the German army had retreated Henri de Man had escaped across the Alps to Switzerland where he lived and wrote until his death in 1953. Paul de Man's new work took him to the United States in 1947 to arrange distribution of books by Éditions Hermès. De Man decided to emigrate to the States but his family were refused an emigration visa because they had no work waiting for them. Instead Anaïde and the children sailed to Argentina, where they stayed with her parents who had recently settled in Buenos Aires. De Man went to New York on a tourist visa, taking up a job as a clerk at the Doubleday bookstore on his arrival and planning to send for his family once he was established.

Although the 'de Man affair' only became a media sensation after de Man's death, in 1955 some information on his wartime writing had been communicated to the faculty at Harvard University, where he was a doctoral student. De Man was asked to explain himself and his letter to the Harvard Society of Fellows forms his only recorded statement on his wartime writing. After acknowledging that his uncle remained 'an extremely debatable case', de Man added, 'I am certainly in no position to pass judgement on him, but I know that his mistakes were made out of a lack of machiavellism and not out of a lack of devotion to his ideals.' He went on to defend himself:

I hear now that I myself am being accused of collaboration. In 1940 and 1941 I wrote some literary articles in the newspaper *Le Soir* and, like most of the other contributors, I stopped doing so when nazi thought-control did no longer allow freedom of statement. During the rest of the occupation, I did what was the duty of any decent person. After the war, everyone was subjected to a very severe examination of his political behaviour, and my name was not a favourable recommendation. In order to obtain a passport, one had not merely to produce a certificate of good conduct, but also a so-called 'certificat de civisme', which stated that one was cleared of any collaboration. I could not possibly have come to this country two times, with proper passport and visa, if there had been the slightest reproach against me. To accuse me now, behind my back, of collaboration, and this to persons of a different nation who cannot possibly verify and appreciate the facts, is a slanderous attack which leaves me helpless.

(Hamacher *et al.* 1989, 477)

De Man's explanation seems to have satisfied Harvard and no more was heard of these allegations until after his death. Conjecture suggests that Harvard's anonymous informant was de Man's first wife, Anaïde Baraghian, from whom he was by then separated.

## READING THE COMPLETE WORKS OF PAUL DE MAN

In the absence of de Man himself to explain his actions it is almost impossible to decide whether he was an opportunist, who made a living by associating his intellectual abilities with everything that we know to be totally unacceptable, or, whether he was merely a naïve fool, too easily influenced by a famous uncle, who was dazzled by the idea of having his own literary column in a national newspaper. Perhaps the truth lies in a peculiar mix of the two. It would certainly be a case of intellectual poverty to imagine that there are only two options. However, it is clear that in de Man's later work he has totally repudiated any of the 'fascistic sympathies' he may have expressed in his wartime writing. In fact, if one wished to look for a connection between his deconstruction and his journalism, one might say that his later work provided him with the intellectual tools to account for and critique the totalitarianism displayed in his earlier writing. In this way, one can suggest that the rigour of de Manian deconstruction comes as a consequence of this early intellectual tragedy. Certainly, de Man's final book, *Aesthetic Ideology*, is a sustained criticism of the sorts of positions on literature and history that he adopted in his wartime journalism. If it were not for the appalling nature of the text 'Les Juifs dans la Littérature actuelle', one might say that de Man's early disgrace had a positive influence on him and has been of significant benefit to literary study because it forced de Man to reconsider all his political and cultural assumptions from the ground up. The consequence of this was his long journey towards deconstruction.

What has troubled so many people, who would otherwise be able to forgive de Man for his youthful indiscretion, is that he never made any mention of his wartime activities during his public career. Given the media frenzy that followed their posthumous publication one can understand why, apart from anything else it might have endangered his right to live and work in America. However, one might also say that for de Man this was a personal tragedy, which he spent the rest of his life working to correct.

I will make no attempt to defend de Man's indefensible texts, youth is not an excuse – other young men and women of 21 fought and died in the resistance while de Man wrote for *Le Soir*. Instead I will offer some observations concerning their relation to reading and to deconstruction. Firstly, the discovery of Paul de Man's early journalism should encourage scholars to read the complete works of Paul de Man. This means the later theoretical texts as well as the *full* range of his wartime writing: the single article 'The Jews in Contemporary Literature' should not stand for the entire life and work of Paul de Man. For a powerful critique of the ideological positions occupied by the earlier texts, one can read the later books. Secondly, as an advocate of deconstruction one should not attempt to protect oneself by trying to protect the reputation of de Man from what constitutes a shameful moment in his writing career. Rather, one should except these texts as errors, or worse, which lead to a profound engagement with the problems of literature, history, and politics. Thirdly, one should not remove these texts from history. Instead, it is necessary to appreciate that Paul de Man was a human being, capable of error, and who changed his mind. In other words, Paul de Man has a history of which these texts are only a part. These texts call for reading. More knowledge will be gained from a detailed study of these texts (and their relation to de Man's later work) than from any amount of angry denunciation.

When reading these texts and commentaries on them one should be wary of reading in bad faith. Paul de Man's contribution to critical theory was to stress that things are never as simple as they first appear. Take this as a rule of thumb when approaching an enormously complicated topic such as the history of occupied Europe. Those who have criticised de Man have tended to take '*The Sound of Music* approach' to history in which there are always clear-cut choices, with 'goodies' and 'baddies'. The banality of everyday life under the Third Reich was quite different, especially where the pressing concerns of economic necessity were involved. One should not think of a straight division between 'resistant' and 'collaborationist' but rather of an economy of collaboration in which everyone – unless they publicly attacked the invaders from street corners, which would result in certain death – was collaborating to a greater or lesser degree. Even those involved in clandestine resistance activities, by day had to get along with the Germans out of financial necessity. Within this economy of collaboration some sins are greater than others, and some of no consequence at all. Readers must decide for themselves where de Man's journalism fits into this scheme. We all hope we would have made the correct decision had we been in the same situation, but we can never know how we might have reacted.

## SUMMARY

In 1987 de Man's reputation was dented when it was discovered that he had, as a young man, written for the collaborationist press in occupied Belgium during the war. For the most part the journalism is innocuous but one text, 'The Jews in Contemporary Literature', stands out as particularly worthy of condemnation. Reaction from the media and critics of deconstruction after the revelation of de Man's past was swift and damning but took little account of what de Man had actually written or the whole of his wartime biography. It is up to the reader to decide as to the degree of de Man's guilt. Many have found it difficult to explain why de Man never spoke publicly about his past as it seems to appear in these texts. However, the views expressed in his wartime journalism were thoroughly repudiated in his mature work.

# AFTER DE MAN

The work, life, and death of Paul de Man have had a profound effect on English studies and in the wider field of critical and cultural theory. The phrase 'after de Man' might be interpreted in a number of ways. There is its literal meaning of the intellectual space of theory and literary studies following the death of Paul de Man, what in temporal terms comes *after* Paul de Man. In this sense this chapter will consider the work of some of the critical thinkers who were taught and trained by de Man: Barbara Johnson, Peter Brooks, and Gayatri Chakravorty Spivak. However, the phrase could also be read as it often appears in Art History, in which one painting is said to be after (in the manner of) a greater or preceding artist: *after* Leonardo. Following this reading the chapter will also be concerned with an example of criticism which is after (in the style of) de Man, Geoffrey Bennington's 1989 essay 'Aberrations: de Man (and) the Machine' which is also a study of the use of machines as a metaphor in de Man's writing. Here Bennington points towards de Man's importance for an entire branch of theoretical inquiry into technology. The final sense in which this chapter will read the phrase 'after de Man' is that of 'after' as an adverb, getting after, or going in search of, Paul de Man. This meaning compels the reader to go after de Man, to pursue his texts in order to understand them. To this end the last section of this chapter will examine J. Hillis Miller's 1987 account of a single paragraph from *Allegories of Reading* as the core of his argument concerning the ethics of reading. Miller's analysis of his friend and colleague's work also combines the three possible interpretations of this chapter title.

## DISSEMINATING DE MAN

It can be argued that academia works in terms of diaspora. The Yale School was important not only because it involved a unique concentration of talented critics in one place, but also because it taught and trained a second generation of literary theorists. In this way, the techniques and practices of the Yale School reproduced themselves and spread out into other universities in North America. This is not so much a matter of perpetuating a family business as a question of 'dissemination' (literally 'scattering'), to use a favourite metaphor of deconstruction. De Man's ideas are not reproduced exactly but diffuse among critics, finding their own routes, scattered in unpredictable and often unconventional ways. The fragmentation which accompanies deconstruction is a dissemination without any assurance of either a centre (the proper or definitive interpretation of de Man's work) or a destination (there is no end to the task of reading de Man, we must constantly be getting after him).

The unpredictable nature of this dispersal is demonstrated by the diverse interests of three of de Man's more prominent students: the feminist (later post-colonialist) Barbara Johnson, the psychoanalytic critic Peter Brooks, and the feminist-Marxist-post-colonialist Gayatri Chakravorty Spivak. Barbara Johnson (who started translating Derrida's book *Dissemination* while still a graduate student under de Man's supervision) has in fact offered a trenchant critique of the Yale School. In her essay 'Gender Theory and the Yale School' she describes the scholars at Yale as a 'Male School' (Johnson 1985, 292). She recounts that on the publication of the volume *Deconstruction and Criticism*, 'several of us – Shoshana Felman, Gayatri Spivak, Margaret Ferguson, and I – discussed the possibility of writing a companion volume inscribing female deconstructive protest and affirmation centring not on Shelley's 'The Triumph of Life' ... but on Mary Shelley's *Frankenstein*' (Johnson, 1985, 102). This monstrous parody was to have been called *The Bride of Deconstruction and Criticism*. Johnson's essay is not naïve enough to believe that de Man and his Yale colleagues have nothing to say on the question of gender. Rather, she deconstructs the texts of de Man and the Yale brotherhood to 'demonstrate that they have had quite a lot to say about the issue, often without knowing it' (102). In this way her essay follows the strategy of de Man's own reading practice and might also be said to be 'after de Man' in the second sense of this phrase discussed above.

Johnson's argument here, and elsewhere in her work, is that gender itself is a trope (see p. 17). It is not something literal (a question of being defined by essential bodily givens) but rather gender has a conceptual history and its values are constructed by an elaborate system of rhetoric. However, while gender is rhetorical, rhetoric (or the philosophical history of rhetoric) is also gendered. For example, Johnson reads de Man reading the eighteenth-century British philosopher John Locke in de Man's essay 'The Epistemology of Metaphor' (from *Aesthetic Ideology*). Locke writes of rhetoric:

> Eloquence, like the fair sex, has too prevailing beauties in it to suffer itself ever to be spoken against. And it is in vain to find fault with those arts of deceiving wherein men find pleasure to be deceived.

De Man quotes this passage as an example of the necessary referential illusion of rhetoric, and goes on to say:

> Nothing could be more eloquent than this denunciation of eloquence. It is clear that rhetoric is something one can decorously indulge in as long as one knows where it belongs. Like a woman, which it resembles ('like the fair sex'), it is a fine thing as long as it is kept in its proper place. Out of place, among the serious affairs of men ('if we would speak of things as they are'), it is a disruptive scandal – like the appearance of a real woman in a gentleman's club where it would only be tolerated as a picture, preferably naked (like the image of Truth), framed and hung on the wall.

> (*AI* 36)

Johnson calls de Man's description of the philosophical tradition as a men's club 'tongue-in-cheek'. However, she also comments that de Man's essay highlights the issue of sexual difference that lurks at the heart of philosophy.

Locke later argues that the nature of language (and therefore rhetoric) is really a question of 'what essence is proper to man?' The way the philosophical tradition understands itself is inflected by figures of gender, from Locke's concentration on 'man' to Kant's discussion of analytic technique as 'tidy critical housekeeping'. For Johnson the value of reading de Man is that he shows the undecideability within this problem – is gender determined by rhetoric or rhetoric by gender – 'is due to the asymmetry of the binary model [see pp. 5–7] that opposes the figural to the proper meaning of the figure' (*AI* 48–9). In other words, Locke's equation of the figure of woman with real women is the result of the logocentric model of philosophy his work participates in. Johnson argues that the philosopher's place is always within, rather than outside of, the structures of language and gender and accordingly, because this is a linguistic predicament, such a place can never be proper or authoritatively absolute. This means that patriarchal structures, like the one that governs philosophy, can be altered. Thus, de Man's rhetorical analysis provides a critical lever for a feminist politics of change.

Johnson, then, wants to pursue a feminist critique of language by getting after de Man: using de Manian analysis, reading de Man's texts, and deconstructing the figure of [de] 'Man'. In a twist, of which de Man would no doubt have approved, Johnson concludes her essay by reading a work by 'a Yale daughter', her own *The Critical Difference*. She says of the readings of canonical literature in this brilliant study, 'no book produced by the Yale School seems to have excluded women as effectively as *The Critical Difference*' (110). Thus, Johnson reads her own feminist deconstruction as an allegory of feminism, a feminism which must by necessity fail to be feminist enough. In this book, and its 'sequel' *A World of Difference*, Johnson provides lucid and accessible accounts of deconstructive reading. They combine a critical-rhetorical reading strategy with a sharp political focus which is as suspicious of the unquestioned assumptions which inform traditional feminism as it is of the exclusion of women from the literary and philosophical canons.

Peter Brooks would not describe his work, in any easy sense, as deconstruction. However, the influence of his tutor de Man on his psychoanalytic criticism is pronounced. De Man never directly discusses Sigmund Freud or psychoanalysis but both his vocabulary and reading strategies are never very far from Freud. For example, in *Allegories of Reading* he suggests that 'literature can be shown to accomplish in its terms a deconstruction that parallels the psychological deconstruction of selfhood in Freud' (*AR* 174). In other words, de Man's reading of the literary (or figural) achieves the same deconstruction of the bourgeois-humanist idea of the unified self as that offered by Freud in psychoanalysis. De Man's proposal that the human self is not the master of language but the product of tropes echoes Freud's 'Copernican revolution', in which the 'discovery' of the unconscious undermined the self's claim to be 'master' in his/her 'own home'. Thus, Freud and de Man are kindred spirits in the deconstruction of the traditional western notion of identity. Peter Brooks combines a de Manian sensitivity to literature and linguistic intricacy with a Freudian analysis of the human subject, nineteenth-century literature, and the discipline of psychoanalysis itself.

His first major study, *Reading for the Plot: Design and Intention in Narrative* (1984), is dedicated to de Man. Amongst a number of strong readings it includes an analysis of the ribbon episode from Rousseau's *Confessions*. Here, Brooks reads Rousseau not as de Man does, with the chain of possession of the ribbon as an exchange of meaning, but in terms of a libidinal economy. Thus, Brooks picks up on de Man's account of the ribbon as a symbol of desire. For Brooks the desire to possess the ribbon (or Marion) is a desire to tell a story. In this way, with a typically de Manian gesture, Brooks reads Rousseau's confession as a narrative about narrative. Just as de Man sees the episode as a confession which fails to confess, Brooks reads it as a story which fails to tell a story because the continued exchange of the ribbon does not allow for closure.

*Reading for the Plot* is an outstanding contribution to the field of narrative theory (sometimes called narratology). Its de Manian rigour, close reading, and detailed attention to theoretical texts helped to move narratology away from a structuralist approach (see p. 53) and into a mode of analysis that was characteristically post-structuralist. Brooks' work was instrumental in furthering a 'deconstructive' account of narrative (think of *Allegories of Reading*) by formalising the idea of 'narrative desire', or, the desire to tell and read stories. *Reading for the Plot* thus facilitated a fruitful area of theoretical endeavour throughout the 1980s, which crossed over between the study of narrative, psychoanalysis, and gender. And even though de Man may not have explicitly discussed either gender or psychoanalysis, we can see his ideas disseminated, or diffused, through the work of his student

Brooks who took de Manian principles into unconventional and unexpected routes. In his essay 'Freud's Masterplot' (contained in *Reading for the Plot*) Brooks provides a sharp, and thoroughly de Manian, account of Freud's *Beyond the Pleasure Principle* (1920). As Barbara Johnson does with gender, so Brooks does with narrative, showing the ways in which narrative as a concept is rhetorically inscribed, while showing that the philosophical history of rhetoric (this time Freud) is constructed like a narrative. Brooks' later book *Body Work: Objects of Desire in Modern Narrative* (1993) carries his diffuse 'de Manian' approach into another rich theoretical field, the body.

Gayatri Chakravorty Spivak's work has opened many doors for post-colonial criticism and for the study of post-colonial writing within the academy. Along with Homi K. Bhabha and Robert Young (two other critics whose work would not have been possible without de Man's version of deconstruction) she has helped to install the insights of deconstruction into the intellectual project of post-colonial theory. Her writing could be described, following Johnson and Brooks, as a reading of race as a trope. Despite what racists (and some 'materialist' post-colonial critics) believe, race is not a given, inscribed in the pigment of the skin. Rather, as a concept it has a textual history in which racism is precisely the logocentric gesture which mistakes the figural for the literal. To offer an example, the idea of Aryan (white) supremacy is not based upon any verifiable fact but on a tropological structure. Like Rousseau's discussions of the primitive who calls strangers 'giants', the word 'Aryan' is a metaphor for the 'fear of difference' on the part of the speaker who identifies with this term and a metonym for a racist ideology employed by its adherents. Aryanism itself has a conceptual history, which cannot be dissociated from the history of western philosophy. Here we might think of texts such as Plato's *Republic*, which makes reference to the lost Aryan people of Atlantis, or Friedrich Nietzsche's notion of the *Übermensch* (superman) in *Thus Spake Zarathustra*.

While Spivak (the translator of Derrida's *Of Grammatology*) is not alone in this deconstruction of race (Henry Louis Gates and Paul Gilroy have also adopted similar de Manian arguments) she is one of the few post-colonial critics to pursue the rhetorical nature of race into the canon of European philosophy. In *A Critique of Postcolonial Reason: Toward a History of the Vanishing Present* (1999), which she dedicates to de Man, Spivak offers an extended analysis of Kant, Hegel, and Marx. In a gesture familiar to both Johnson and Brooks, Spivak attempts to show that the philosophical canon is structured by the use of racial tropes, while also suggesting that race itself is a philosophically determined trope. Just as Johnson found the very problem of language and rhetoric to be inflected by questions of gender, so Spivak reads the issue of aesthetics as one determined by race. She writes of her own attempt to read Kant in terms of a racial logic:

> In his analysis of Rousseau, de Man has shown how the discovery that something that claims to be true is a mere trope is the first (tropological) step in what de Man called deconstruction. The second (performative) step is to disclose how the corrective impulse within the tropological analysis is obliged to act out a lie in attempting to establish it as the corrected version of truth. De Man tracked the laying out of this double structure in a handful of writers: Rousseau, Nietzsche, Hölderlin, Proust, Yeats. In Kant, it is the presupposition of the nascent axiomatics of imperialism that gives the tropological deconstruction the lie.
>
> (Spivak 1999, 18–19)

Spivak follows de Man into the text of Kant and in this way continues the work started by de Man in *Aesthetic Ideology*. Spivak differs from her fellow 'siblings' Johnson and Brooks in terms of her attachment to a certain idea of Marxism and in this respect may be even closer to de Man's final work than has hitherto been imagined.

Unlike Johnson, Spivak does not explicitly address the texts of de Man. Instead de Man's influence can be felt in the texts Spivak reads and the way she reads them. Like Johnson, Spivak's work is obviously political, in a way that has not always been appreciated about de Man's own writing. In an interview she states:

> People like us learned [from Paul de Man] the predicament of discovering an aporia [see p. 87] in a text, and then moved in other directions with the aporetic structure. Whereas, since he was articulating it, it took him a long time establishing it in text after text. ... [Instead] read him with a new politics of reading ... where he suggests that in order to act you turn the metaphor, you literalize the metaphor, then he's out of simply articulating aporias. This is the work he

was on when he died: the work of moving from the description of tropological and performative deconstruction to a definition of the act.

(Spivak 1990, 107–8)

In so far as post-colonial theory explicitly attempts to formulate the conditions of thought for political actions, Spivak is continuing the later work of de Man in *Aesthetic Ideology*. It is an irony that while – following the revelation of his wartime journalism – his own texts have come in for rebuke and censure as apolitical, his influence is all pervasive in the theoretical enterprise most commonly associated with political action.

## THE TEXT AS MACHINE

Much of the commentary on de Man after 1987 has tended to mull over the question of the political, or otherwise, nature of his writing. Discussion has been divided along predictable lines with de Man's admirers and friends defending his reputation, while those with an historical axe to grind against deconstruction have inevitably repeated their traditional criticisms of de Man and the Yale School. In fact, it could be argued that the trauma experienced by the field of deconstruction in the wake of the 1987 revelations served to concentrate the minds of de Man's attentive readers on the political implications of his rhetorical strategy. Sean Burke argues in *The Death and Return of the Author* (1998) that the de Man affair effectively changed the direction of theoretical inquiry in the English-speaking academy. He argues that the simple notion of 'the death of the author' (itself a misreading of Roland Barthes' essay of the same name, not to be found anywhere in the work of Paul de Man) had to be rethought following the questions of authorship, responsibility, and ethics raised by the discovery of de Man's wartime journalism. Geoffrey Bennington has always been an astute reader of 'the politics of deconstruction'. One such example is his essay 'Aberrations: de Man (and) the Machine', in *Reading de Man Reading* (1989). Here he argues that de Man's writing is inextricably bound up with the political and the ethical:

De Man's readings generate ethical preoccupations that they cannot dominate: they do this not through any lack of rigour, but because of their rigour. To

suggest that de Man's work is somehow reprehensibly apolitical is therefore
blindly superficial.

(220)

Bennington suggests that de Man – unlike his detractors – was aware
that adopting a political or ethical position, however necessary, be it for
or against Paul de Man, is not enough to come to terms with the
nature of ethics or politics. Such an understanding requires rigorous
thinking and a sustained reading of philosophy.

However, Bennington's interest in this essay lies in the questions of
technology and literature as a machine, which have subsequently
become significant areas of theoretical inquiry in their own right.
Bennington reads de Man's essay 'Pascal's Allegory of Persuasion', in
*Aesthetic Ideology*, through an earlier passage from *Allegories of Reading*.
He notes that while traditional literary studies habitually deplores the
language of machines (reading or writing 'mechanically' is considered
something negative) de Man sets out a theory of the text as machine in
the final section of *Allegories*. De Man writes:

> The machine is like the grammar of the text when it is isolated from its rhet-
> oric, the merely formal element without which no text can be generated. There
> can be no use of language which is not, within a certain perspective thus radi-
> cally formal, i.e. mechanical, no matter how deeply this aspect may be
> concealed by aesthetic, formalistic delusions. ... The text as body, with all its
> implications of substitutive tropes ultimately always retraceable to metaphor,
> is displaced by the text as machine and, in the process, it suffers the loss of the
> illusion of meaning. The deconstruction of the figural dimension is a process
> that takes place independently of any desire; as such it is not unconscious but
> mechanical, systematic in performance but arbitrary in its principles, like a
> grammar. ... Far from seeing language as an instrument in the service of a
> psychic energy, the possibility now arises that the entire construction of drives,
> substitutions, repressions, and representations is the aberrant, metaphorical
> correlative of the absolute randomness of language, prior to any figuration or
> meaning.

(*AR*, 294, 298, 299)

Like many of the appreciative accounts of de Man after his death,
Bennington's essay is an attempt to come to terms with the rigour and
density of de Man's final writing through the possibility that the

arguments outlined in the later texts are already present within the earlier monographs.

Bennington argues that the idea of the machine is a threatening one because it has a relation to death. A machine that can operate by itself implies the death (or absence) of its inventor and user. The use of machines as labour-saving devices is, according to Freud, a consequence of the death instinct, which seeks to bring human activity to a state of absolute rest. Machines repeat and repetition is also linked in psychoanalysis to compulsive behaviour and so to the desire for death. Therefore, when de Man adopts the metaphor of the text as machine in his conclusions to *Allegories of Reading* it has profound significance for literary studies. What is at stake here is not 'the death of the author', de Man always maintained that Rousseau and Proust in a 'technical' (this mechanical term is used deliberately here) sense always knew what they were doing when they set up texts which deconstructed themselves. Rather, for Bennington, the problem of reading itself is the issue here. For the radical formality of the text as machine (a text which is 'programmed' to self-deconstruct without the intervention of a reader) implies not the death of the author but the death of the reader.

If the text is bound to deconstruct its own assumptions and values, it does so in a way that is both systematic (it has been programmed to happen) and arbitrary (independent of any attempt to programme the deconstruction by a reader). The text therefore generates its own meaning independent of its readers (including its first reader, the author). De Man concludes that this is indicative of 'the absolute randomness of language, prior to any figuration or meaning'. Bennington suggests, however, that this is an example of 'aberration' in de Man's own writing. 'Aberration', one of de Man's favourite words in *Allegories*, takes place, says Bennington, 'whenever one of a series of elements is also used transcendentally with respect to that series in order to totalize, dominate, or explain it' (216). For example, the idea that Marxism as one theory among many can explain the history of all theories, or, that philosophy as one discipline among many is the best discipline because it can subsume or explain all the other disciplines. Similarly, of all the metaphors that de Man uses to describe the action of texts he finally privileges the idea of the machine even though it is just one metaphor in a series of metaphors. This is not an 'aberration' is the sense that it is a wild error, rather it is a consequence of the mechanical nature of language which de Man's metaphor describes.

De Man's own reading throws up aberrations like this one, just as, say, Rousseau's texts arbitrarily generate meanings which they cannot control (the insistence of offering a confession while simultaneously demonstrating the impossibility of confession is a good example). For Bennington, such aberration is itself an ethical issue because 'it signals the unavoidability of attempting to resolve ethical and political questions either cognitively [by thought] or performatively [by action], and the equally unavoidable irreducibility of such questions to the terms of truth or performativity' (220). In other words, the categories of the political and the ethical cannot be understood outside of or anterior to their inscription in tropes and rhetoric. As such, both the political and ethical will be affected by the radical formality of the text as machine and the technical aberrations of language. For example, in voting we attempt to resolve ethical and political questions, after some thought, through a performative act. However, if this act of voting did in fact resolve those questions there would be no need to vote ever again or to continue worrying about ethics and politics. We know that this is not the case and that the nature of the political and ethical cannot be reduced to, or resolved by, the performance of a vote. Instead, 'the political' and 'the ethical' are themselves concepts caught up in the rhetorical structure of language. When after much consideration we actually vote, this choice is an 'aberration' in de Man's sense because it privileges one term with respect to a series of choices. We make our choice in an attempt to dominate that series – the party I choose will do the best job – even though this choice cannot be transcendental with respect to the series. The 'truth' of the voter's choice cannot be verified outside of the text of political discourse (claim and counterclaim, spin and counter-spin) and so cannot totalise or dominate the series of voting choices. As such, democracy is a linguistic predicament.

## THE ETHICS OF READING

As Bennington's essay suggests, the question of the ethics of reading has, following de Man's death, become a central concern for literary theory. This concentration on ethics is in part intended by some as a corrective to the alleged irresponsibility and ambivalence of Yale School deconstruction. The argument runs: how can anyone suggest that death is only 'a displaced name for a linguistic predicament' (*RR*

81, see pp. 78–9)? This is unethical, death is a serious business. As we have seen such objections are based on non-reading and selective misquotation. De Man on this singular occasion is discussing the figure of death in a particular text by Wordsworth not World War II, as his critics would have us believe. J. Hillis Miller's study *The Ethics of Reading* (1987) was written before the discovery of de Man's early journalism and effectively argues that the question of ethics is paramount to de Man's rhetorical analysis.

By the phrase 'the ethics of reading' Miller means that aspect of reading in which the reader makes a response to a text that is both necessary (in that it is a response to an irresistible demand) and free (in that the reader takes responsibility for their response and for the effects – institutional, political, historical – of their reading). Miller argues that 'what happens when I read *must* happen, but I must acknowledge it as *my* act of reading' (43). Ethics is this unconditional obligation to read and to take responsibility for the effects of that reading. One might argue that a text like 'The Jews in Contemporary Literature' is unethical because while it may only say what it says in order to protect its author's livelihood, it does not take responsibility for the anti-Semitic consequences it might produce in the real world.

However, the mature de Man repudiates such positions and is well aware of the ethical consequences of reading. Miller builds his argument around a passage from *Allegories of Reading*:

> Allegories are always ethical, the term ethical designating the structural inter-ference of two distinct value systems. In this sense, ethics has nothing to do with the will (thwarted or free) of a subject, nor *a fortiori*, with a relationship between subjects. Morality is a version of the same language aporia that gave rise to such concepts as 'man' or 'love' or 'self', and not the cause or the consequence of such concepts. The passage to an ethical tonality does not result from a transcendental imperative but is the referential (and therefore unreliable) version of a linguistic confusion. Ethics (or, one should say, ethicity) is a discursive mode among others.

> (*AR* 206)

We should be familiar by now with the logic of this extract from our understanding of *Allegories* (see chapter 2). De Man rejects the conventional understanding of ethics as an act of free will by a conscious and unified subject who knows what is ethical before s/he makes a decision. Instead, the idea of 'morality' or 'the ethical' is a concept, which both has a philosophical history and is a trope sustained by a metaphorical-metonymical structure. Ethics, like the political, religious, or literary texts de Man analyses in *Allegories* is just one 'discursive mode among others' rather than a regulatory rule for all language. Morality only exists inside of human discourse, never outside of it. Accordingly, ethical pronouncements are subject to the same rhetorical complications as other uses of language and so will always fail to be ethical enough. We might say that such texts can only ever be allegories of ethics.

This is not to dismiss the idea of ethics but finally to think through ethics as a conceptual, rather than a transcendental, problem. De Man argues that the word 'reading' bars 'access, once and forever, to a meaning that yet can never cease to call out for understanding' (*AR* 47). In other words, the moment we give a name to the act of reading, the logocentric inscription 'reading', this term will always be inadequate to describe the complex phenomenon it designates. Our understanding because it is linguistic must be limited, but reading remains to be understood and is in de Man's estimation the only thing worth understanding. We continue to read but we cannot fully think through (understand) what it is we are doing. One of the ways in which we place limits on our ability to understand reading, says Miller, is by making ethical judgements and demands.

Ethical judgements such as 'this book is good/bad/should be banned/should be published' have no foundation in knowledge about the text. Such knowledge, like the text, is linguistic and so cannot be verified within itself as either true or false (we might recall that Rousseau's inability to confess in his text is based on a similar problem). However, language demands that we make such pronouncements, in so far as these tropes (true/false, right/wrong) impose themselves in any use of language. There could be no use of language outside of an idea of right/wrong and true/false even if such terms have no authoritative grounding in a use of language. A user of language must attempt to make that language refer to ideas and things in the world, they have no choice. Therefore, s/he must presuppose an idea of true and false even if language is insufficient to verify the values of true and false. Thus we must make ethical pronouncements just as those statements must remain linguistic and so ungrounded. This is what de Man means when he calls ethics 'the structural interference of two distinct value systems' (*AR* 206): the referential and the linguistic.

There is then no escape from making ethical judgements and demands (they are unconditional) while at the same time they cannot dominate reading because they are part of the reading process. As Miller argues, both the failure of ethical demands to dominate a text and their unwarranted affirmation 'are *bound* to take place, since both are inscribed within the text as its own failure to read itself' (54). Miller's essay might be said to be 'after de Man' not only because he studies a text by de Man, but in so doing his patient and detailed reading relentlessly pursues the meaning of that text, doing justice to its sophistication in the same way that de Man reads others. It is a profound irony that following his death de Man has been criticised by means of an approach to reading – ethics – which he himself initially formulated, without those critics appreciating the complexity of the issue in which they are engaged. The ethical critique of de Man, problematically, takes no account of the inability of such value judgements to dominate the texts they dismiss. It is for this reason that critics of de Man would be better advised to read his texts rather than to denounce them. By 'read' here I do not mean reading in the narrow sense of picking up a text and gleaning meaning from it. Rather, I mean de Man's understanding of reading as a way of critically interpreting the world and the texts that comprise it. As such reading is an ethical and political activity and if we were all to read 'after de Man' (in the style of de Man) we might go some way to understanding the intractable political and ethical problems that shape our world.

In conclusion, Paul de Man's life and work have had a profound impact on literary studies and critical theory. While at Yale he trained a generation of thinkers who later went on to occupy some of the most prestigious academic posts in America. Consequently, his ideas have been disseminated (scattered) among a number of important theoretical areas, including: feminism, narratology, post-colonialism, and Marxism. His death, and the events that followed it, has also left its mark on the academy. As a supposed corrective to the perceived irresponsibility of Yale School deconstruction, the agenda of theoretical inquiry has shifted from linguistic analysis to an investigation of issues such as politics and ethics. However, as sensitive readers of de Man's own texts have shown such questions were always central to de Man's thinking anyway.

# APPENDIX

## 'The Jews in Contemporary Literature'

## Paul de Man, *Le Soir*, 4 March 1941

Vulgar anti-Semitism willingly takes pleasure in considering post-war cultural phenomena (after the war of 14–18) as degenerate and decadent because they are *enjuivé* [enJewished]. Literature does not escape this lapidary judgement: it is sufficient to discover a few Jewish writers under Latinised pseudonyms for all of contemporary production to be considered polluted and evil. This conception entails rather dangerous consequences. First of all, it condemns *a priori* a whole literature which in no way deserves this fate. What is more, from the moment one agrees that the literature of our day has some merit, it would be a rather unflattering appreciation of western writers to reduce them to being mere imitators of a Jewish culture which is foreign to them.

The Jews themselves have contributed to spreading this myth. Often, they have glorified themselves as the leaders of literary movements that characterise our age. But the error has, in fact, a deeper cause. The very widespread belief, according to which the modern novel and modern poetry are nothing but a kind of monstrous outgrowth of the world war, is at the origin of the thesis of a Jewish take-over. Since the Jews have, in fact, played an important role in the artificial and disordered existence of Europe since 1920, a novel born in this atmosphere would merit, up to a certain point, the qualification of *enjuivé*.

But the reality is different. It seems that aesthetic evolutions obey very powerful laws, which continue their action even when humanity is shaken by considerable events. The world war provoked a profound upheaval in the political and economic world. But artistic life has been stirred relatively little and the forms that we know today are the logical and normal consequences of what was there before.

This is particularly clear where it concerns the novel. Stendhal's definition, according to which 'the novel is a mirror carried along a highway', carries within it the law which still governs this literary genre today. There was first the obligation to respect external reality scrupulously. But by digging deeper, the novel has began to explore psychological reality. Stendhal's mirror no longer stays immobile the length of the road: it undertakes to search even the most secret corners of the souls of characters. And this domain has shown itself to be so fruitful in surprises and riches that it still constitutes the one and only terrain of investigation of the novelist.

Gide, Kafka, Hemingway, Lawrence – one could extend the list indefinitely – all do nothing but attempt to penetrate, according to characteristic methods, into the secrets of interior life. Through this attribute, they show themselves to be, not innovators who have broken with all past traditions, but mere continuers who are only pursuing further the realist aesthetic that is more than a century old.

An analogous demonstration could be made in the domain of poetry. The forms that seem to us most revolutionary, like surrealism or futurism, in fact have orthodox ancestors from which they cannot be detached.

Therefore, one may see that to consider contemporary literature as an isolated phenomenon created by the particular mentality of the 20s is absurd. Similarly, the Jews cannot claim to have been its creators, nor even to have exercised a preponderant influence over its development. On any close examination, this influence appears even to have extraordinarily little importance since one might have expected that, given the specific characteristics of the Jewish spirit, the latter would have played a more brilliant role in this artistic production. Their intellectualism, their capacity to assimilate theories while keeping a certain indifference [*froideur*] in the face of them, seemed to be very precious qualities for the work of lucid analysis demanded by the novel. But in spite of that, Jewish writers have always been of secondary importance and, to speak only of France, the André Mauroises, the Francis de Croissets, the Henri Duvernoises, the Henri Bernsteins, Tristan

Bernards, Julien Bendas, and so forth, are not among the most important figures, nor are they especially those who have had any guiding influence on the literary genres. The observation is, moreover, comforting for western intellectuals. That they have been able to safeguard themselves from Jewish influence in a domain as representative of culture as literature is proof of their vitality. We would have to give up hope for its future, if our civilisation had let itself be invaded by a foreign force. By keeping, in spite of Semitic interference in all aspects of European life, an intact originality and character, it has shown that its basic nature is healthy. Furthermore, one sees that a solution of the Jewish problem* that would aim at the creation of a Jewish colony isolated from Europe would not entail, for the literary life of the west, deplorable consequences. The latter would lose, in all, a few personalities of mediocre value and would continue, as in the past, to develop according to its great evolutive laws.

Translated Martin McQuillan

---

*    Despite its shocking appearance this does not refer to 'the final solution' of the Holocaust – the article is dated too early for that – but to a plan discussed at an international conference on refugees in 1938, on the initiative of the American President Roosevelt, to resettle displaced German Jews on the African island of Madagascar. This idea was later discussed with Hitler by Pope Pius XII, as well as the French and British governments.

# FURTHER READING

## WORKS BY PAUL DE MAN

Complete bibliographies of individual essays by de Man can be found in *The Resistance to Theory* (*RT* 122–7) and in De Graef 1995 (255–62).

*Blindness and Insight: Essays in the Rhetoric of Contemporary Criticism*, 2nd edition (Minneapolis: University of Minnesota Press, 1983).

De Man's first collection of essays, discussed in chapter 1 of this book. Originally published in 1971 and revised in 1983 (with five additional essays), it contains essays ranging from 1955 to 1971. This book is one of the early attempts to mark out literary theory as a field of inquiry by taking critical texts, rather than literary ones, as its object of study. Its primary interest lies in the hypothesis that critical texts are paradoxically blind at the points where they are most insightful. However, it is also of interest in tracing the passage of ideas through de Man, from readings of New Criticism to engagements with deconstruction.

*Allegories of Reading: Figural Language in Rousseau, Nietzsche, Rilke, and Proust* (New Haven and London: Yale University Press, 1979).

The only full monograph study by de Man published during his lifetime (discussed in chapter 2 of this book). Its radical understanding of language and literature brought de Man to international recognition, while its elaboration of a rhetorical deconstruction lead to, often acrimonious, controversy within the academy. In a nutshell it argues that every text is an allegory of its own misreading and that all language (not just literature) is figural. In this way, meaning is said to be arbitrary and beyond the control of the reader as well as the author. It introduces the important idea that texts deconstruct themselves. The essay on Proust and Part 2 on Rousseau are among the finest critical writing of the century.

Bloom, Harold, Paul de Man, Jacques Derrida, Geoffrey Hartman and J. Hillis Miller, ed., *Deconstruction and Criticism* (New York: Seabury Press, 1979).

The volume that established the Yale School as an important site of theoretical inquiry in America. It contains de Man's essay 'Shelley Disfigured' as well as texts by Bloom, Derrida, Hartman, and Miller. Worth reading to distinguish between the various approaches of the individual members of the school as they all provide different readings of Shelley's 'The Triumph of Life'. Derrida's important text 'Living On: Borderlines' is split in two, with his reading of Shelley on the top half of the page and a series of comments on methodological issues in deconstruction running along a border at the bottom.

*The Resistance to Theory* (Minneapolis: University of Minnesota Press, 1986).

A posthumous collection of essays (discussed in chapter 3 of this book) from the period after *Allegories of Reading*. It opens with the essay 'The Resistance to Theory' which argues that the interest of literary theory lies in its own impossibility. This provocative essay set the tone for the theory wars, which shook up the humanities during the 1980s. The volume also includes essays on Walter Benjamin, Reader-Response Theory, Mikhail Bakhtin, deconstruction, and semiotics. It concludes with a rare interview by de Man in which he discusses his final unfinished project on Marx. Contains an impressive bibliography of texts by de Man.

*The Rhetoric of Romanticism* (New York: Columbia University Press, 1984).

This collection of mature essays (discussed in chapter 4 of this study) demonstrates de Man's fascination with Romantic literature. It furthers the arguments made about language in *Allegories*, while deepening de Man's understanding and use of deconstruction. The essays 'Autobiography as De-Facement', 'Wordsworth and the Victorians' and 'Shelley Disfigured' stand out as excellent examples of de Man's critical strategy during his Yale School years. The book also contains readings of Rousseau, Hölderlin, Yeats, and Kleist.

*Wartime Journalism, 1939–1943*, ed. Werner Hamacher, Neil Hertz and Thomas Keenan (Lincoln: University of Nebraska Press, 1988).

Contains all of the wartime journalism rediscovered by Ortwin de Graef after de Man's death (discussed in chapter 7 of this book). The essays appeared in their original languages, some in French (*Le Soir*) and some in Flemish (*Het Vlaamsche Land*). This happened for two reasons: firstly, so that readers could come to terms with what de Man had actually written without the mediation of errors in translation, secondly, in order to publish the material as quickly as possible. Had the incident occurred today the Internet may have been the chosen medium to ensure quick access for all to these texts. On the whole the essays themselves are unremarkable reviews of Flemish culture of the period and would be of little interest beyond the fact that they were written by de Man. However, a few texts stand out as more engaged with the German occupier than one would have hoped for from de Man. In particular the essay 'The Jews in Contemporary Literature' has dealt de Man's personal reputation a severe blow and given many an excuse to dismiss the radical implications of his later work.

*Critical Writings: 1953–1978*, ed. Lindsay Waters. (Minneapolis: University of Minnesota Press, 1989).

Another posthumous collection – this time of early essays by de Man. The collection provides an important link between de Man's wartime journalism and his first significant study *Blindness and Insight*. It includes a number of essays written before de Man began the professional study of literature as an academic. While the volume might be said to represent a 'pre-deconstructive' de Man, the rigour of his thinking and his keen literary ear are both in evidence through out. Lindsay Waters makes a convincing case in her introduction for reading the essay 'The Inward Generation', collected here, as symptomatic of de Man's mourning for his wartime errors.

*Romanticism and Contemporary Criticism: The Gauss Seminar and Other Papers*, ed. E.S. Burt, Kevin Newmark, and Andrzej Warminski (Baltimore: Johns Hopkins University Press, 1993).

As the title suggests this volume is a mix of essays on Romantic literature and contemporary critical texts. It is divided into three parts. The first contains six essays from the Gauss seminar given by de Man at Princeton University in 1967. Like the first three essays in Part 2 on Romantic topics written between 1954 and 1965, the Gauss seminar presents a de Man closer to the earlier texts in *Blindness and Insight* than to his mature voice in *Allegories*. The other essay in Part 2 is a fascinating account of Roland Barthes commissioned in 1972 by the *New York Review of Books* but never published. The third part of the collection presents two responses to papers given at conferences in the 1980s by the critics Frank Kermode and Murray Krieger.

*Aesthetic Ideology*, ed. Andrzej Warminski (Minneapolis: University of Minnesota Press, 1996).

The final volume of posthumously collected essays (discussed in chapter 6 of this book) which draws together de Man's last work on aesthetics and politics. The essays here are among de Man's most difficult but their patient study will bear rich rewards. The readings of European philosophy contained in this book might be thought of as staging posts toward de Man's proposed account of Marx and Kierkegaard as the two key readers of Hegel in the philosophical tradition. These essays make little reference to deconstruction and hint at de Man emerging from the shadow of the Yale School to stake a claim as a leading thinker of the century. Sadly, de Man died before developing these essays into a complete study.

## WORKS ON PAUL DE MAN

Brooks, Peter, Shoshana Felman, and J. Hillis Miller, eds, *The Lessons of Paul de Man* (New Haven: Yale University Press, 1986).

A collection of memorial texts for de Man – started life as a special edition of *Yale French Studies*, 69, 1985. Provides an insight into de Man's critical achievement by detailing the high regard in which colleagues and students held him. The sense of loss expressed by the contributors is no doubt heightened by the context of institutional debates about deconstruction – emphasises the importance of de Man as a teacher.

Cohen, Barbara, J. Hillis Miller, Andrzej Warminski, and Tom Cohen, ed., *Material Events: Paul de Man and the Afterlife of Theory* (Minneapolis: University of Minnesota Press, 2000).

An exciting new collection of essays by a number of leading commentators within deconstruction, including: Michael Sprinker, Laurence Rickels, J. Hillis Miller, Ernesto Laclau, Judith Butler, and Jacques Derrida. The essays address the political implications of de Man's final texts, concentrating on his notion of the materiality of language. This book begins the task of thinking seriously about de Man's work, now that the agitation of the theory wars and the 'de Man affair' have subsided.

De Graef, Ortwin, *Serenity in Crisis: A Preface to Paul de Man, 1939–1960* (Lincoln: University of Nebraska Press, 1993) and *Titanic Light: Paul de Man's Post-Romanticism, 1960–1969* (Lincoln: University of Nebraska Press, 1995).

De Graef's mature reflection on the early life and career of Paul de Man. In contrast to much of the media frenzy that surrounded de Graef's initial discoveries, these volumes are rigorous in their criticism and thorough in their reporting of de Man's biography. De Graef argues that de Man's texts from the wartime journalism onwards are persistently concerned with the question of history. Excellent bibliographies of the complete works of Paul de Man.

Hamacher, Werner, Neil Hertz and Thomas Keenan, *Responses: On de Man's Wartime Journalism* (Lincoln: University of Nebraska Press, 1989).

Extraordinary collection of essays from the field of deconstruction following the revelation of de Man's wartime journalism, contributors include: Rodolph Gasche, Peggy Kamuf, Richard Klein, J. Hillis Miller, Samuel Weber, Herman Rappaport, and Jacques Derrida. Despite claims often made against this book, these essays are not an attempt to 'deconstruct' (i.e. explain away) de Man's error. Rather, they unequivocally condemn de Man while trying to think through the problems posed by the existence of his wartime journalism. Reading this book can be a deeply moving experience.

Derrida, Jacques, *Memoirs for Paul de Man*, revised edition (New York: Columbia University Press, 1989).

Originally published in 1986, containing three lectures given in memory of de Man, later revised to include Derrida's reflection on the wartime journalism, 'Like the Sound of the Sea Deep within a Shell'. Only, this edition contains the complete text of this later essay. The original essays are an act of remembrance for de Man but they also trace the figure of memory through de Man's writing. Derrida makes interesting comments on a range of topics including narrative and the question of deconstruction in America.

Derrida, Jacques, *Of Grammatology*, trans. Gayatri Chakravorty Spivak (Baltimore: Johns Hopkins University Press, 1974).

According to one recent reviewer this book has a claim 'to being among the most devastating texts to have appeared this century' (Royle 1997, 393). It is quite simply the most important and influential book published in the humanities since the war. It lays out an incredibly ambitious line of argument, which proposes the deconstruction of the whole of western thought. Its argument and relation to de Man are discussed in chapter 1 of this book.

Gasché, Rodolph, *The Wild Card of Reading: On Paul de Man* (Cambridge, Mass.: Harvard University Press, 1998).

A demanding but very rewarding study of de Man's rhetorical reading strategy. Gasché is arguably the most rigorous thinker in deconstruction today and he affords considerable insight into de Man's work. He argues that de Man is best read through the texts of Kant, Hegel, and Derrida, while distinguishing between de Man and Derrida's deconstruction. Gasché also expresses reservations about some of the philosophical manoeuvres in de Man's essays.

Johnson, Barbara, *The Critical Difference: Essays in the Contemporary Rhetoric of Reading* (Baltimore: Johns Hopkins University Press, 1980) and *A World of Difference* (Baltimore: Johns Hopkins University Press, 1987).

These volumes combine brilliant readings of literature and elegant expositions of theoretical problems by a 'Yale daughter'. The first essay in *The Critical Difference*, 'Rigorous Unreliability', is an accessible and stimulating account of de Man's critical approach. Her essay 'On Apostrophe and Abortion', in *A World of Difference*, is a superb analysis of political undecideability in relation to rhetoric. Johnson's mediation between Jacques Derrida and the psychoanalyst Jacques Lacan, around their readings of the Edgar Allan Poe story 'The Purloined Letter', 'The Frame of Reference: Poe, Lacan and Derrida' (in *The Critical Difference*), is justly considered a classic account of deconstruction.

McQuillan, Martin, ed., *Deconstruction: A Reader* (Edinburgh: Edinburgh University Press, 2000).

This volume offers a selection of texts from the field of deconstruction in all its radical diversity, including work by Paul de Man. It examines the fortunes of the term deconstruction, and the ideas associated with it, in the work of the leading commentators on Derrida's texts. It covers a broad range of topics, including: Aids, architecture, art, feminism, ghosts, law, Marxism, postmodernism, race, revolution, Shakespeare, technology, theology, and telepathy. The editor's introduction provides a useful elaboration of a number of the issues raised by this book.

Miller, J. Hillis, *The Ethics of Reading: Kant, de Man, Eliot, Trollope, James, and Benjamin* (New York: Columbia University Press, 1987).

Miller's pre-'de Man affair' consideration of ethics as a concern in *Allegories of Reading* (discussed in 'After de Man', this book). Miller combines a Yale School accuracy with his own accessible expository style, taking the reader through de Man's argument step by step. Of particular interest is the way in which Miller situates de Man's approach to ethics in terms of both philosophy (Kant and Benjamin) and literature (Eliot, Trollope, and James).

Norris, Christopher, *Paul de Man: Deconstruction and the Critique of Aesthetic Ideology* (New York: Routledge, 1988).

Accessible and lucid early attempt to account for de Man's theory of aesthetic ideology, while the relevant essays were still in periodical form. However, Norris follows the path of de Man's reflection on politics and the aesthetic from the 1950s onwards, providing a detailed exposition of the full range of de Man's career. The writing of this book was interrupted by the revelation of de Man's wartime journalism and concludes with an urgent attempt to address them.

Salusinsky, Imre, *Criticism in Society: Interviews* (London: Methuen, 1986).

An important collection of interviews from the 1980s, it helped to introduce American critical practices to the rest of the world. The book includes interviews with Jacques Derrida, Harold Bloom, Geoffrey Hartman, J. Hillis Miller, and Barbara Johnson amongst others. Each interview concludes with a reading by the interviewee of a poem by Wallace Stevens, 'Not Ideas about the Thing but the Thing Itself'. The late Paul de Man is fondly remembered in these texts, while Barbara Johnson provides a fascinating account of life as a graduate student at Yale.

Waters, Lindsay and Godzich, Wlad, *Reading de Man Reading* (Minneapolis: University of Minnesota Press, 1989).

Remains, perhaps, the most thorough and illuminating over-view of de Man's work. Includes essays from: Geoffrey Hartman, Carol Jacobs, Peggy Kamuf, J Hillis Miller, Werner Hamacher, Bill Readings, Rodolphe Gasché, and Geoffrey Bennington (discussed in 'After de Man', this book). It also contains another essay by Derrida on de Man, 'Psyche: Inventions of the Other'. The collection covers a range of material from history and politics to machines and children. However, the volume attempts to discuss de Man's understanding of reading as a theoretical problem.

# WORKS CITED

Note: Works by Paul de Man which are cited in this book are listed in the Further Reading section.

Althusser, Louis (1977) 'Ideology and Ideological State Apparatus' (1969), in *Lenin and Philosophy and Other Essays*, trans. Ben Brewster, 2nd edition (London: New Left Books).

Benjamin, Walter (1992) 'The Task of the Translator', in *Illuminations*, ed. Hannah Ardent, trans. Harry Zohn (London: HarperCollins).

Bennington, Geoffrey (1989) 'Aberrations: de Man (and) the Machine', in Waters, Lindsay and Godzich, Wlad, *Reading de Man Reading* (Minneapolis: University of Minnesota Press).

Bloom, Harold (1973) *The Anxiety of Influence: A Theory of Poetry* (New York: Oxford University Press).

—— (1975) *A Map of Misreading* (New York: Oxford University Press).

Brooks, Peter (1984) *Reading for the Plot: Design and Intention in Narrative* (New York: Knopf Press).

—— (1993) *Body Work: Objects of Desire in Modern Narrative* (Cambridge, Mass.: Harvard University Press).

Burke, Sean (1998) *The Death and Return of the Author: Criticism and Subjectivity in Barthes, Foucault and Derrida*, 2nd edition (Edinburgh: Edinburgh Unversity Press).

De Graef, Ortwin (1995) *Titanic Light: Paul de Man's Post-Romanticism, 1960–1969* (Lincoln: University of Nebraska Press).

Derrida, Jacques (1989) *Memoirs for Paul de Man*, revised edition (New York: Columbia University Press).

—— (1992) 'Force of Law: the Mystical Foundation of Authority', in *Deconstruction and the Possibility of Justice*, edited by Drucilla Cornell, Michel Rosenfeld, and David Gray Carlson (New York: Routledge), pp. 3–67.

Eagleton, Terry (1983) *Literary Theory: An Introduction* (Oxford: Blackwell).

Freud, Sigmund (1920) *Beyond the Pleasure Principle*, in *The Standard Edition of the Complete Psychological Works*, ed. J. Strachey (London: Hogarth Press, 1953), Vol. 18, pp. 1–64.

Hamacher, Werner, Neil Hertz and Thomas Keenan (1989) *Responses: On de Man's Wartime Journalism* (Lincoln: University of Nebraska Press).

Johnson, Barbara (1985) 'Gender Theory and the Yale School', in Robert Con Davis and Ronald Schleifer, ed., *Rhetoric and Form: Deconstruction at Yale* (Norman: University of Oklahoma Press), pp. 101–12.

Miller, J. Hillis (1987) *The Ethics of Reading: Kant, de Man, Eliot, Trollope, James, and Benjamin* (New York: Columbia University Press).

Nietzsche, Friedrich (1980) 'On Truth and Lie in an Extra-Moral Sense', in *The Portable Nietzsche*, ed. Walter Kaufmann (New York: Random).

Royle, Nicholas (1997) 'Phantom Review', *Textual Practice*, 11(2): 386–98.

Spivak, Gayatri Chakravorty (1990) 'Practical Politics of the Open End', in *The Post-Colonial Critic: Interviews, Strategies, Dialogues* (London: Routledge), pp. 99–111.

Spivak, Gayatri Chakravorty (1999) *A Critique of Postcolonial Reason: Toward a History of the Vanishing Present* (London and Cambridge, Mass.: Harvard University Press).

Waters, Lindsay and Wlad Godzich (1989) *Reading de Man Reading* (Minneapolis: University of Minnesota Press).

# INDEX

performative 38, 123
Phenomenology 15
philosophy 32–3
plastic arts 52
Plato 118
politics 32, 83–91, 123
post-colonialism 51, 126
Poulet, Georges 24
presence 6, 26
promises 39–40, 56
prosopopeia 77–9
Proust, Marcel 32, 34, 35–6, 75, 122, 132
psychoanalysis 51, 116–18

reader-response theory 15, 16, 54, 132
reading 13, 18, 19–21, 54, 124–6
Readings, Bill 91
rhetoric 14, 17–19, 20, 32, 41, 115
Riffaterre, Michael 14
Rilke, Rainer Maria 32
Romantic literature 3, 32, 65–79
Rousseau, Jean-Jacques 8, 14, 21, 23, 24–8, 31, 37, 38–46, 54, 56, 57, 58, 67, 68–9, 72, 75, 86, 117, 122, 123, 132, 133

Schiller, Friedrich 81, 94, 95
sexual difference 115
Shakespeare, William 70
Shelley, Mary Wollstonecraft 66, 114–15
Shelley, Percy Bysshe 66–72, 74, 76, 114, 132

Smith, Adam 89
sociology 86
Spanish Civil War 100
Spivak, Gayatri Chakravorty 1, 113, 114, 118–20, 136
*Star Wars* 76–7
Steiner, George 14
structuralism 15, 53

text 23, 36–7, 38–40, 56, 57, 122
*Textual Practice* 97
theory wars 3, 50
totalisation 77
totalitarianism 96
translation 58–64

undecideability 55, 87

Voltaire, François-Marie Arouet de 67

Waters, Lindsay 133, 138
Weber, Max 59
Weber, Samuel 97–8, 135
Wordsworth, William 66, 72–9
writing 21–2, 25, 35

Yale School 8, 9, 66, 98, 114–15, 120, 123, 126
Yale University 2, 4, 8
Yeats, William Butler 3, 133
Young, Robert 118

Zohn, Harry 60, 61